WHERE THE NATIVES FEAST IN NEW ORLEANS

...a Secret Guide to Local Restaurants

by

Jamie Menutis

&

Debby Hirsch Wood

WHERE THE NATIVES FEAST IN NEW ORLEANS

. . . a Secret Guide to Local Restaurants

To order this book, write neworleansdining@aol.com; see our website at www.nativesfeast.com.

First Printing 2002
Hauser Printing Co., Inc.
5720 Heebe Street
Elmwood Business Park
Harahan, Louisiana 70123

DEDICATION

Jamie Menutis

This book is dedicated to my parents for teaching me optimism and my daughter Ana Sofia for teaching me love.

Debby Wood

I dedicate this book to my tender husband, Donald who afforded me the opportunity to be a full-time mom and have spare time to write this book. I equally dedicate this book to my three loved and creative children, Tiffany, Hunter, and Emily.

ACKNOWLEDGEMENTS

Heartfelt thanks go to Marika Marcello for her artistic talents in creating our fantastic cover. We also thank our dining out friends who so eagerly shared their favorite places with us. Further, we express gratitude to the many restaurant owners and chefs for letting us into their kitchens and sharing with us their zest for great food.

Map provided courtesy of
Map New Orleans, Inc.
504-891-0990
www.mapneworleans.com
Get your copy of the New Orleans Street Map
& Visitor Guide today!

ABOUT THE AUTHORS

A New Orleans native, Jamie's life loves include her gorgeous daughter Ana Sofia, traveling the world in a moment's notice, political discussions that last throughout the night, listening to Blues and opera, and, of course, great wine, and food anywhere in the world. Jamie has a Master of Arts Degree in International Affairs from Georgetown University and has worked on political and human rights policy in Washington, DC, Vienna, Austria, and in East and West Africa. Jamie and her daughter currently live in New Orleans and eat out as much as possible.

With New Orleans jazz in her genes, Debby has been a long-time resident of the Crescent City. Her interests include enjoying the music of Sergei Rachmaninoff, Richard Wagner, David Benoit, and EarthSuit, scuba diving in places like the Red Sea with her husband Donald, traveling, studying health and nutrition, running, discussing politics, religion, and history with intelligent friends over a delicious dinner, and loving every moment of her childrens' lives. Debby has a Master of Fine Arts Degree from Tulane University in Piano Performance. She oversees her childrens' lessons and activities and is in her Suburban way too much.

INTRODUCTION

Putting into words the enthusiasm that native New Orleanians have when asked about their favorite local restaurants is a daunting task. First, you'd better have time to listen, because their favorites are never limited to only one or two places. Secondly, if you're going to write a book about New Orleans restaurants, you should have an idea about how many you are going to feature. Also, listening to a local describe their favorite restaurant in New Orleans is like listening to someone tell you about the time they went sky diving or saw Jimi Hendrix live at Woodstock. Their words are full of adrenaline and their mouths don't stop moving.

During the research phase of the book, we literally listened to locals describing their favorite places to eat for months (after all, there are over 3,000 restaurants in this City). This part was a lot of fun because it meant talking with so many people about something truly great in our City. Our job then became to re-describe, with local flair and language, places that New Orleanians seem to agree upon most for their favorite places to eat and produce a guidebook that was truly useful and unique. However, before we could write about the restaurants, we needed to eat at just a few more places! How else could we really call ourselves "true guide-book writers" without having tried every restaurant on the list? A few pounds later, we finally completed the task. One thing is for certain, we have always taken for granted the great food that makes our City famous. We grew up thinking that similar food was pretty much a universal given. Now we have grown wiser to that notion and also prouder. Not only does New Orleans offer a great number of world famous restaurants that are true gems, but literally there are thousands of "lesser known" places that are its backbone and sources of culinary inspiration. This book is a tribute to those "lesser known" places that we can't live without and whose existence make New Orleans the culinary place that it is. Thanks to the people of New Orleans who are enthusiastic and excited about great eating as their number one agenda.

On a purely business note, we have attempted to furnish the most up-to-date and accurate information concerning each establishment. However, as you know in the restaurant world, menus, chefs, operating hours, and owners often change. It is always a good practice to call ahead before going to any restaurant. We've listed the phone numbers for this purpose. Please know that we are not trying to trick you if your experience does not match ours. Tastes and opinions are subjective but we are confident that you will agree with us for the most part on our selections.

We are also interested in hearing about your experience and hope that our book inspires you to become a proactive diner by recording your dining experiences on the journal pages included behind each restaurant. And for those that are of hardy spirit and love experiencing the flavors of New Orleans, try our traditional New Orleans recipes we have offered in our book. In this way, you bring New Orleans cooking right into your own home. Please feel free to correct us on information and send us your comments or suggestions at neworleansdining@aol.com.

Continue the journey of great eating!

Jamie Menutis
Debby Wood
January 1, 2002

Table of Contents

Location

Maps

to

Where the Natives Feast

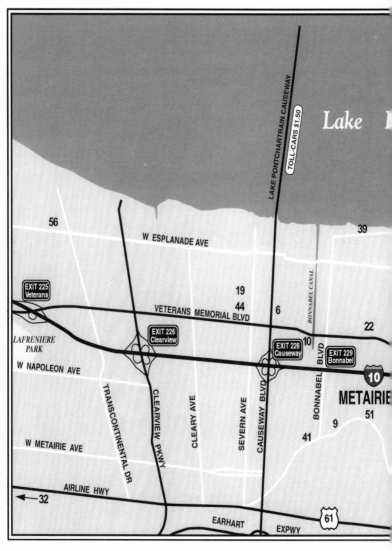

1. Acme Oyster & Seafood House
2. Angelo Brocato's Ice Cream & Confectionery
3. Barataria
4. Basil Leaf
5. Bon Ton Cafe
6. Bozo's
7. Brigtsen's
8. Bruning's Seafood Restaurant
9. Byblos Lebanese Cuisine
10. Byblos Market
11. Café Atchafalaya
12. Café Giovanni
13. Christian's
14. Clancy's
15. Cuvée Restaurant

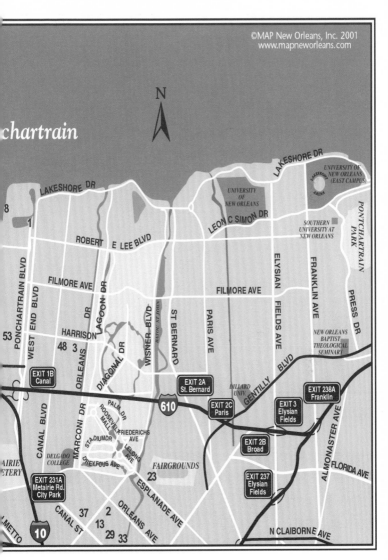

©MAP New Orleans, Inc. 2001
www.mapneworleans.com

16. Deanie's Seafood
17. Dick and Jenny's
18. Dooky Chase's
19. Drago's
20. Feeling's Café D'Aunoy
21. Five Happiness
22. Fury's Restaurant
23. Gabrielle Restaurant

24. Gautreau's Restaurant
25. Genghis Khan
26. Irene's Cuisine
27. Jacques-Imo Café
28. Jamila's Café
29. Katie's
30. Kelsey's Restaurant
31. La Crepe Nanou

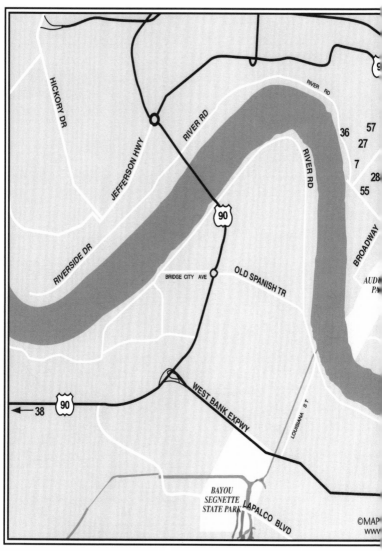

32. Le Parvenu Restaurant
33. Liuzza's Restaurant & Bar
34. Mandich Restaurant and Bar
35. Mandina's Restaurant
36. Mat & Naddie's Cafe
37. Michael's Mid City Grill
38. Mosca's

39. Mr. Ed's Seafood & Italian Restaurant
40. Nautical
41. Odyssey Grill
42. Peristyle
43. Pho Tau Bay Restaurant
   (Westbank)
44. Pho Tau Bay Restaurant
   (Metairie)

4

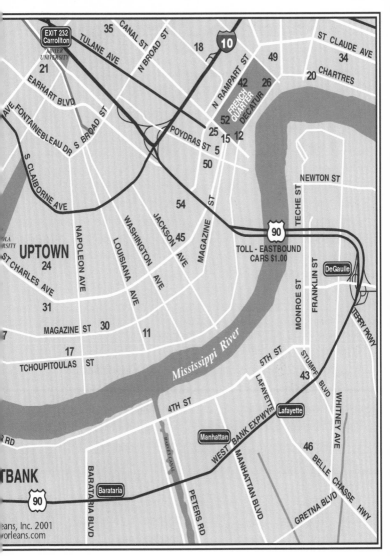

Favorite Local Restaurants

Acme Oyster & Seafood House
Acropolis Cuisine
All Natural Foods and Deli
**Angelo Brocato's Ice Cream
    & Confectionery**
Bank's Street Grill
Barataria
Basil Leaf
Bayona
Bennachin
Bluebird Café
Bombay Club
Bon Ton Café
Bozo's
Bravo Italian Kitchen
Brigtsen's
Bruning's Seafood Restaurant
Bud's Broiler
Byblos Lebanese Cuisine
Byblos Market
Bywater BBQ
Café Atchafalaya
Café Degas
Café Giovanni
Café Marigny
Café Rani
Café Sbisa
Café Volage
Caffe Caffe
Chateaubriand Steak House
Camellia Grill

Chez Nous Charcuterie
China Blossom
China Rose
Christian's
Clancy's
Clover Grill
Cuvée Restaurant
Deanie's Seafood
Dick and Jenny's
Domilise Sandwich Shop
    & Bar
Dooky Chase's
Drago's
Eleven 79
Elizabeth's
Fausto's Bistro
Feeling's Café D'Aunoy
Figaro's Pizzerie
Five Happiness
Foodies Kitchens
Fury's Restaurant
Gabrielle Restaurant
Galatoire's
Gamay Bistro & Bar
Gautreau's Restaurant
Genghis Khan
GW Fin's
Herbsaint
Hernandez Cafeteria in the
    Hale Boggs Federal
    Building

* Bold – see text for more detailed description.

Favorite Local Restaurants

Igor's Buddha Belly Bar
Igor's Garlic Clove
   Restaurant
Il Tony's Italian Restaurant
   and Seafood
Indigo Restaurant
Irene's Cuisine
Jacques-Imo Café
Jamila's Café
Jerusalem Restaurant
Joey K's Restaurant & Bar
Johnnie's Po-Boys & Caterer
Katie's
Kelsey's Restaurant
Kim Son Restaurant
La Crepe Nanou
La Cuisine
La Marquise Pastry Shop
La Provence
La Riviera Restaurant
La Spiga Bakery
Landry's Restaurant
Lemon Grass Restaurant
Le Parvenu Restaurant
Liborio's Cuban Restaurant
Liuzza's Restaurant & Bar
Lola's
Mande's Restaurant
Mandich Restaurant and Bar
Mandina's Restaurant

Mark Twain's Pizza
   Landing
Martin Wine Cellar
Mat & Naddie's Cafe
Maximo's Italian Grill
Maspero's
Metro Bistro
Michael's Mid City Grill
Midnight Express Café
Mona's Café
Mo's Riverbend Café
Mosca's
Mother's
**Mr. Ed's Seafood & Italian
   Restaurant**
Mr. Gyro's Greek Food
Mulate's
Nautical
New City Diner
New York Pizza
Nine Muse's
Nine Roses
Nirvana Indian Cuisine
Odyssey Grill
Orient Dong Phuong
   Restaurant
Pampy's Steak & Seafood
   Grill
Parasol's
Pascal's Manale
Peristyle

* Bold – see text for more detailed description.

Favorite Local Restaurants

Pete's Deli
Pho Tau Bay
Pontchartrain Bistro and Wine Bar
Port of Call
Portobello Café
Pupuseria Divino Corazon
R&O Pizza Place
Red Room
Red Sea Restaurant
Reginelli's Pizzeria
Restaurant des Familles (Crown Point, LA)
Riccobono's Panola Street Café
Rio Mar
Ristorante Carmelo
Rock-n-Sake Bar & Sushi
Rocky & Carlo's
Royal Blend Coffee & Tea
Royal China Restaurant
Saia's Beef Room
Sake Café
Sal & Judy's
Santa Fe
Sclafani's
Semolina's
Sid-Mar's of Bucktown
Smilie's Restaurant
Stella!

Superior Grill
Taj Mahal Indian Cuisine
Taqueria Corona
Taqueros
Tavern on the Park
The French Table
The Galley Seafood Restaurant
The Pelican Club
The Po-Boy Bakery
The Sporting House Café
The Steak Knife Restaurant & Bar
Tony Angello's Restaurant
Trey Yuen Cuisine of China
Tujague's
Uglesich Restaurant & Bar
Upperline Restaurant
Vaqueros
Vega Tapas Café
Venezia
Vera Cruz
Vic's Kangaroo Café
Victor's
Vincent's Italian Cuisine
Wasabi
West End Café
Wolfe's
Ye Olde College Inn
Zachary's Restaurant

* Bold – see text for more detailed description.

Favorite Local Restaurants by Neighborhood

CENTRAL BUSINESS DISTRICT

Bon Ton Café
Chez Nous Charcuterie
Cuveé Restaurant
Eleven 79
Genghis Khan
Hernandez Cafeteria in the Hale Boggs Federal Building
Cafeteria
Igor's Buddha Belly Bar
Joey K's Restaurant & Bar
Lemon Grass Restaurant
Liborio's Cuban Restaurant
Metro Bistro
Mother's
Mulate's
New City Diner
Nine Muse's
Nine Roses
Nirvana Indian Cuisine
Pete's Deli
Royal Blend Coffee & Tea
Taqueria Corona
The Sporting House Café
Uglesich Restaurant & Bar
Victor's

FAUBOURG MARIGNY

Feelings Café D'Aunoy
La Spiga Bakery
Mona's Café
Wasabi

FRENCH QUARTER

Acme Oyster & Seafood House
Bayona
Bombay Club
Café Giovanni
Café Marigny
Café Sbisa
Clover Grill
Deanie's Seafood Restaurant
Galatoire's
Gamay Bistro & Bar
GW Fin's
Irene's Cuisine
Johnnie's Po Boys & Caterer
La Marquise Pastry Shop
Maspero's
Maximo's Italian Grill
Midnight Express Café
Mr. Gyro's Greek Food
Peristyle
Port of Call
Ristorante Carmelo
Santa Fe
Sclafani's in New Orleans East
Stella!
The Pelican Club
Tujague's

LAKEFRONT / LAKEVIEW / BUCKTOWN

Acme Oyster & Seafood House (Lakefront)
Barataria (Lakeview)
Bruning's Seafood Restaurant (West End)
China Rose (Lakefront)
Deanie's Seafood Restaurant (Bucktown)
Il Tony's Italian Restaurant and Seafood (Bucktown)
La Cuisine (Lakeview)
Landry's Restaurant (Lakeview)
R&O Pizza Place (Bucktown)
Reginelli's Pizzeria (Lakeview)
Russell's Marina Grill (Lakefront)
Sid-Mar's of Bucktown (Bucktown)
The Steak Knife Restaurant & Bar (Lakeview)
Tony Angello's Restaurant (Lakeview)
West End Café (Lakefront)
Wolfe's (Lakefront)

METAIRIE / OLD METAIRIE / KENNER

Acropolis Cuisine
Bozo's
Bravo Italian Kitchen
Byblos Lebanese Cuisine
Byblos Market
Caffe Caffe
Drago's
Fausto's Bistro
Foodies Kitchens
Fury's Restaurant
La Riviera Restaurant
Mark Twain's Pizza Landing
Martin Wine Cellar
Mr. Ed's Seafood & Italian Restaurant
Odyssey Grill
Pho Tau Bay
Portobello Café
Royal Blend Coffee & Tea
Royal China Restaurant
Saia's Beef Room
Sake Café
Semolina's International Pasta
Taj Mahal Indian Cuisine
Taqueria Corona
Taqueros
The French Table
The Galley Seafood Restaurant
Vega Tapas Cafe
Vincent's Italian Cuisine

MID-CITY / CARROLLTON

Angelo Brocato's Ice Cream & Confectionery
Bank's Street Grill
Basil Leaf
Bennachin
Brigtsen's
Bud's Broiler
Café Degas
Chateaubriand Steak House
Christian's
Dooky Chase's
Five Happiness
Gabrielle Restaurant
Jerusalem Restaurant
Katie's
Liuzza's Restaurant & Bar
Lola's
Mandina's Restaurant
Michael's Mid City Grill
Mo's Riverbend Café
Tavern on the Park
Venezia
Ye Olde College Inn

UPTOWN

All Natural Foods and Deli
Bluebird Café
Bravo Italian Kitchen
Café Atchafalaya
Café Rani
Café Volage
Camellia Grill
Clancy's
Dick and Jenny's
Figaro's Pizzerie
Gautreau's Restaurant
Herbsaint
Igor's Garlic Clove Restaurant
Jamila's Café
Jacques-Imo Café
Kelsey's Restaurant
La Crepe Nanou
Mat & Naddie's Cafe
Mona's Café
Nautical
New York Pizza
Parasol's
Pascal's Manale
Pontchartrain Bistro and Wine Bar
Red Room
Riccobono's Panola Street Café
Rock n Sake Bar & Sushi
Superior Grill
Taqueria Corona
Upperline Restaurant
Vaqueros
Vera Cruz
Vincent's Italian Cuisine

NEAR AND NOT-SO-NEAR RESTAURANTS

Bywater BBQ (Bywater)
Elizabeth's (Bywater)
Catfish Charlie's (Hammond)
La Provence (Northshore)
Mandich Restaurant and Bar (Bywater)
Mosca's (Avondale)
Orient Dong Phuong Restaurant (New Orleans East)
Pampy's Steak & Seafood Grill (Gentilly)
Pho Tau Bay (Gretna)
Pupuseria Divino Corazon (Gretna)
Red Sea Restaurant (Earhardt Blvd.)
Restaurant des Familles (Crown Point, LA)
Rocky & Carlo's (Chalmette)
Sal & Judy's (Lacombe)
Sclafani's (New Orleans East)
Smilie's Restaurant (Jefferson)
Taqueria Corona (Harahan)
The Po-Boy Bakery (Gentilly)
Trey Yuen Cuisine of China (Mandeville, Hammond)

MY NEW ORLEANS DINING JOURNAL

<u>ACME OYSTER & SEAFOOD HOUSE</u>

Date & Time:_____Total Expense: _____

Companion(s):_____

Description of décor:_____

Directions to restaurant
and parking information:_____

_____

Service:_____

Favorite Food(s)/Wine(s):_____

_____

_____

_____

_____

My remarks and
impressions:_____

_____

_____

_____

SAVE BUSINESS CARD OR RESTAURANT SOUVENIR HERE

ACME OYSTER & SEAFOOD HOUSE

724 Iberville Street
New Orleans, LA 70130
(504) 522-5973

7306 Lakeshore Drive
New Orleans, LA 70124
(504) 282-9200

519 East Boston Street
Covington, Louisiana 70433
(504) 898-0667

Inexpensive

Acme Oyster House first opened its doors in 1910 and continues to win awards for the best raw oysters, po-boys[1], and seafood dishes. With three locations going strong in 2001, Acme shows no sign of slowing down. Though most people are familiar with the French Quarter location, my absolute favorite Acme is on Lakeshore Drive. The restaurant there is much larger and the atmosphere more relaxed than the Quarter location. You can dine outdoors on the veranda overlooking Lake Pontchartrain on nice days (and nights). I also find it a child-friendly place (my daughter and I love to sit outside and order crab claws!). Many single diners like to sit around the bar where they can get a bite to eat, socialize, and catch a game on the tube.

Acme is a place where oyster enthusiasts like to set oyster consumption records. I think 37 dozen is a recent record I was told! Acme offers a number of New Orleans specialties like gumbo poopa, red beans or white beans and rice (with choice of three types of sausages), jambalaya, oyster bisque, as well as seasonal, boiled seafood, and po-boys. Of course, if you like oysters, you might as well order a dozen while you're there. They also offer a new creation: *Cajun Sushi* – raw and fried oyster and shrimp creations with pressed rice and green onions. Acme offers up local hospitality, great seafood traditions, and good service.

---

[1] New Orleans' version of the submarine sandwich served on French bread.

MY NEW ORLEANS DINING JOURNAL

ANGELO BROCATO ICE CREAM & CONFECTIONERY

Date & Time:_____Total Expense: _____

Companion(s):_____

Description of décor:_____

Directions to restaurant
and parking information:_____

_____

Service:_____

Favorite Food(s)/Wine(s):_____

_____

_____

_____

_____

My remarks and
impressions:_____

_____

_____

_____

SAVE BUSINESS CARD OR RESTAURANT SOUVENIR HERE

ANGELO BROCATO
ICE CREAM & CONFECTIONERY

214 North Carrollton Avenue
New Orleans, Louisiana 70119
486-1465

Mid-City
Inexpensive

This rare and Sicilian-authentic Italian ice cream and pastry shop is a third generation, family owned confectionery. In 1905, Angelo Brocato — after an apprenticeship in Palermo, Italy — came to America and established his own ice cream parlor that epitomizes the old-world, old-fashioned and unpretentious ice cream store of ages past.

I have no will power when it comes to Brocato's spumoni ice cream, almond macaroons, almond crescents, or fig cookies. You can enjoy your favorite "gelatos" (Italian ice cream) made daily in flavors such as lemon (only lemon, sugar and water), strawberry, mango, orange, amaretto, or pistachio nut under the lazy ceiling fans as your eyes feast on the numerous Italian cakes and cookies (that you can't pronounce) that await selection. You may want to try the baked Alaska, nucotoli (almond spice cookies), sesame seed cookies, as well as Italian ice cream sodas and coffee. Brocato's has a tradition of using quality ingredients in their family recipes including fresh cream and fruit (fig trees abound in New Orleans). This is a splurge worth taking and the calories are justified (and besides most of the ice creams are ices!). If for some reason you miss a trip to this quaint pâtisserie, you may find the spumoni ice cream at Save-a-Center or Winn Dixie. Many locally-owned grocery stores such as Dorignacs, Langenstein's, and Zuppardos also carry bags of Brocato's wonderful Italian cookies. Either way, Brocatos is a highly valued emblem among New Orleanians.

MY NEW ORLEANS DINING JOURNAL

<u>BARATARIA</u>

Date & Time:_____Total Expense: _____

Companion(s):_____

Description of décor:_____

Directions to restaurant
and parking information:_____

_____

Service:_____

Favorite Food(s)/Wine(s):_____

_____

_____

_____

_____

My remarks and
impressions:_____

_____

_____

_____

SAVE BUSINESS CARD OR RESTAURANT SOUVENIR HERE

BARATARIA

900 Harrison Avenue
New Orleans, Louisiana 70124
(504) 488-7474

Lakeview
Moderate

As the restaurant's name implies, Barataria references food caught in Louisiana's Barataria Bay rich with oysters, fish, crabs, and shrimp. This informal, comfortably and softly lit (with white table cloths) local restaurant has oysters year round (due to the fact that they are cultivated and harvested for its customers from Louisiana oyster beds from the same family for over 60 years). Needless to say, you will find a fantastic array of appetizers and entrees (for lunch or dinner) like chateaubriand for one bordelaise, jerked, blackened, au poivre (peppered with green peppercorn sauce), seafood bouillabaisse (oyster, scallops, crab, and shrimp), fried oysters, oysters with fresh spinach and herbsaint, rack of lamb (with smoked bacon demi-glace), grilled shrimp and asparagus salad, and sautéed baby veal with oysters, garlic, tomato, in a meunier butter sauce.

Chefs Thomas Daussat and Peter Everett create cuisine at Barataria with Creole overtones and a classic French influence. The steaks are great here — I get mine with the peppercorn sauce. The paneed veal comes with angel hair bordelaise, lamb, chicken, or scallops. For those of you that thrive on garlic, try the Ralphie bread or anything with the "Ralphie sauce." You can get the Ralphie vegetable bread (with spinach, artichoke, pepper, onion, black olive, tomato, and marinara); Ralphie bread steak (with onion, pepper, blue cheese, mushroom, and demi-glace); Ralphie Bread shrimp, or Ralphie bread oyster (with garlic, Romano cheese, tomato and spinach). You'll adore the bold flavor, and once is not enough — you will look forward to your next meal at Barataria (as the flavor of the Ralphie sauce will haunt you until you return for another fix). The service staff is extremely friendly (they know most of their customers by their first names) and knowledgeable of the menu and how things are prepared. This cozy Lakeview neighborhood restaurant poses as a fine five-star restaurant without all the pomp.

MY NEW ORLEANS DINING JOURNAL

BASIL LEAF

Date & Time:_____Total Expense: _____

Companion(s):_____

Description of décor:_____

Directions to restaurant
and parking information:_____

_____

Service:_____

Favorite Food(s)/Wine(s):_____

_____

_____

_____

_____

My remarks and
impressions:_____

_____

_____

_____

SAVE BUSINESS CARD OR RESTAURANT SOUVENIR HERE

BASIL LEAF

1438 South Carrollton Avenue
New Orleans, Louisiana 70118
(504) 862-9001

Uptown
Moderate

Of all the dining experiences in New Orleans, the Basil Leaf stands out as innovative, sophisticated, and exotically "the best" Thai place to eat in the City. The Chef, Siam Titiparwat creates imaginative, orchestrated cuisine, fresh and full of flavor. This bistro — with lots of windows, overlooks the streetcar line on Carrollton Avenue and has an extensive Thai menu, including lemon shrimp salad, basil-crusted sea scallops, mee grob (roasted shrimp and chicken sautéed with vegetables in spicy wine sauce over crispy noodles), and sesame-coated soft-shell crab. The presentations are chic and are a delight to the eye like a colorful painter's palate.

The food is healthful with lots of vegetarian entries from which to choose like sautéed veggies and Thai curry – served with Jasmine rice and angel hair pasta with tofu, shitake mushrooms and vegetables. Your mind and stomach will be happy here. Don't forget to try the Thai Tea – an imported blend of oak and spice flavors bringing you to another country in just one sip. Overall, Basil Leaf will fully satisfy your curiosity for Thai cuisine (this is not a place for those of you that like meat and potatoes — sorry). If you are adventuresome and willing to try exotic curry sauces, try grandmother's hot sauce or sticky rice with flan, you will thoroughly enjoy the experience and meal at Basil Leaf.

MY NEW ORLEANS DINING JOURNAL

BON TON CAFE

Date & Time:_____Total Expense: _____

Companion(s):_____

Description of décor:_____

Directions to restaurant
and parking information:_____

_____

Service:_____

Favorite Food(s)/Wine(s):_____

_____

_____

_____

_____

My remarks and
impressions:_____

_____

_____

_____

SAVE BUSINESS CARD OR RESTAURANT SOUVENIR HERE

BON TON CAFÉ

401 Magazine Street
New Orleans, Louisiana 70130
(504) 524-3386

Downtown
Moderate to Expensive

Five words describe the Bon Ton Café - locally loved and historically Cajun. The Bon Ton Café has been a popular favorite since the 1900's — housed in the historical 1840's Natchez building not far from the Mississippi River. Its atmosphere is energetic and cheerful (probably similar to the attitude of the Cajuns that came to Louisiana from their home in Canada). The Bon Ton Café fames itself as the oldest existing Cajun restaurant (where the head chefs have a combined 60 years of experience!). Typically "Cajun" cuisine relies on the foods from Louisiana's bayous and the Gulf of Mexico such as crawfish éouffée, crawfish bisque, soft shell crab, redfish, lump crabmeat, and shrimp and oyster jambalaya. The Bon Ton Café's authentic tradition of true Cajun cooking has inspired many chefs in restaurants across the nation and the Bon Ton Café has branded its name in many international culinary societies, gourmet publications as well as travel and leisure magazines.

No matter what you order — it will be consistently delicious and fresh. The proprietors, Wayne and Debbie Pierce, have guarded Bon Ton's recipes given by their ancestors who lived deep in the Cajun country of LaFourche and Terrebonne Parishes. Must tries are the shrimp remoulade (with Alzina's homemade remoulade sauce), all étouffées, the soft shell crab Alvin (topped with crabmeat, together with French fried onion rings), fried trout, crawfish bisque, fried shrimp with homemade tartar sauce and/or homemade cocktail sauce, or the crabmeat salad. You won't want to miss trying the Rum Ramsey Cocktail or Bon Ton's homemade bread pudding with Whisky sauce. This is a very popular place for downtown executives to dine for lunch. You won't get any more authentically Cajun food unless you get into a pirogue with Boudreaux on the bayou.

MY NEW ORLEANS DINING JOURNAL

BOZO'S

Date & Time:_____Total Expense: _____

Companion(s):_____

Description of décor:_____

Directions to restaurant
and parking information:_____

_____

Service:_____

Favorite Food(s)/Wine(s):_____

_____

_____

_____

_____

My remarks and
impressions:_____

_____

_____

_____

SAVE BUSINESS CARD OR RESTAURANT SOUVENIR HERE

BOZO'S

3117 21st Street
Metairie, Louisiana 70002
(504) 831-8666

Metairie
Moderate

Most of us (as well as our parents) have had the pleasure of knowing and going to Bozo's most all of our lives. This restaurant began in 1928 and has continued to be a favorite in the local scene. The very friendly Chef Chris Vodanovich and his family own and operate this fine seafood restaurant. I met Mr. Chris ("Bozo") as a young girl while dividing up fried shrimp and catfish with members of Pete Fountain's band. My dad was a jazz musician and played the xylophone with Mr. Fountain for many years. Mr. Chris would make sure that everyone dining there was more than happy.

Mr. Chris has found the secret to frying catfish – (after all he sure has had time to – 20 years of frying in his present location). Many claim that Bozo's has the best fried catfish in the New Orleans area. Wonderful raw oysters, gumbo (made fresh daily), boiled shrimp and boiled crawfish (roll up your sleeves) are standards on the menu (when they are in season). Before your meal arrives, make certain that you peek at the kitchen through its large window and you probably will see Mr. Chris frying fish in a neat, clean kitchen.

Bozo's is open for lunch and dinner except for Sunday and Monday. Bozo's is a great place to relax with friends, a cold draft, and leisurely eat a great tasting meal.

MY NEW ORLEANS DINING JOURNAL

<u>BRIGTSEN'S</u>

Date & Time:_____Total Expense: _____

Companion(s):_____

Description of décor:_____

Directions to restaurant
and parking information:_____

_____

Service:_____

Favorite Food(s)/Wine(s):_____

_____

_____

_____

_____

My remarks and
impressions:_____

_____

_____

_____

SAVE BUSINESS CARD OR RESTAURANT SOUVENIR HERE

BRIGTSEN'S

723 Dante Street
New Orleans, Louisiana 70118
(504) 861-7610

Uptown
Expensive

Brigtsen's is a premiere, upscale restaurant loved by locals for many years. Chef/owner Frank Brigtsen has won numerous awards including the recent *Restaurant & Institutions* magazine's Ivy Award. The dining area includes three cozy and intimate rooms that speak of warmth and style . . . but atmosphere is secondary to the fantastic presentation and gastronomic delights.   You'll never tire of Brigtsen's menu because it's always re-inventing itself.

On our last visit we enjoyed the sautéed sweet-breads with mashed potatoes, shitake mushrooms, capers and lemon-roasted garlic sauce as an appetizer. For a main course, we favored the grilled beef tornedos with tasso Marchand de Vin sauce and Bleu cheese (how great was this . . . melt in your mouth great! I wanted to give the Brigtsen's a hug).   Debby had the stuffed veal with shitake mushrooms and Brie red pepper corn sauce (she recently became a vegetarian, well, you know it must have been good!). You can also choose from a numerous array of creative dishes such as butternut shrimp bisque soup, rabbit tenderloin on an andouille Parmesan grits cake with spinach and creole mustard sauce, broiled Gulf fish with crabmeat Parmesan crust, mushrooms, and béarnaise. Whatever you order will reflect the talents, vision, and signature of Chef Brigtsen. We toured the small kitchen and were surprised that such a tiny space could produce so many wonderful meals! If you can only go to one restaurant in New Orleans, we suggest you make Brigtsen's the one.

MY NEW ORLEANS DINING JOURNAL

BRUNING'S SEAFOOD RESTAURANT

Date & Time:_____Total Expense: _____

Companion(s):_____

Description of décor:_____

Directions to restaurant
and parking information:_____

_____

Service:_____

Favorite Food(s)/Wine(s):_____

_____

_____

_____

_____

My remarks and
impressions:_____

_____

_____

_____

SAVE BUSINESS CARD OR RESTAURANT SOUVENIR HERE

BRUNING'S SEAFOOD RESTAURANT

1924 West End Parkway
New Orleans, Louisiana 70124
(504) 282-9353

West End
Inexpensive to Moderate

This five-generation old restaurant run by the Bruning family first opened its doors in 1859. Bruning's specializes in serving seafood that is exclusively native to Lake Pontchartrain, Lake Borgne, and the Gulf of Mexico. Situated on Lake Pontchartrain in West End Park, Bruning's quickly rebuilt its temporary restaurant in a building that they owned located just in front of the original restaurant when Hurricane Andrew destroyed the original structure.

Bruning's menu changes with the season's offerings for its fish and crayfish; they let you know the right time to order the best crayfish, oysters, or redfish. There's an oyster bar, of course, and seafood comes as you like — fried or broiled. Hard crabs can be ordered by the half or full dozen, as well as crayfish and boiled shrimp. Whole flounder comes broiled, fried or stuffed. There is also a children's menu and one for those with "light" appetites. The oyster and soft-shell crab po-boys are great, as is the seafood platter that offers a variety of Louisiana-grown seafood cooked to order. From the bar, you can order a traditional New Orleans drink such as a Sazerac, Mint Julip, or Bruning's signature drink "The Lakesider" — a cranberry, pineapple, and orange drink combined with Puerto Rican rum. For dessert, Bruning's offers its own bread pudding or sugar-free cheesecake.

MY NEW ORLEANS DINING JOURNAL

BYBLOS LEBANESE CUISINE

Date & Time:_____Total Expense: _____

Companion(s):_____

Description of décor:_____

Directions to restaurant
and parking information:_____

_____

Service:_____

Favorite Food(s)/Wine(s):_____

_____

_____

_____

_____

My remarks and
impressions:_____

_____

_____

_____

SAVE BUSINESS CARD OR RESTAURANT SOUVENIR HERE

BYBLOS LEBANESE CUISINE

1501 Metairie Road
Metairie, Louisiana 70005
(504) 834-9773

Old Metairie
Inexpensive to Moderate

Truly Lebanese, Byblos is a refreshingly ideal neighborhood restaurant found in wonderful Old Metairie. After a warm, family welcome from owner/general manager Tarek Tay, you will see about 16 tables in a relatively intimate setting with delightfully hand-painted floral murals reminiscent of a Lebanese town. As you peruse the menu, you will find appetizers like hummus, baba ghanuj (eggplant dip), lentil stew, eggplant stew, stuffed cabbage rolls, spinach pie, stuffed grape leaves, and labneh (Lebanese cream cheese topped with olive oil and dried mint). My favorite salads are the tabbouleh, Greek, and yogurt.

The house specialties are authentically Lebanese (as well as everything at Byblos) and mouthwatering (and good for you!). Byblos has this exotic way of putting things on a kabob – like lamb skewered with vegetables and charbroiled, pork tenderloins, shrimp (lightly marinated in extra virgin olive oil, herbs and spices and then charbroiled), beef (with onions, parsley and Lebanese spices on skewers and charbroiled), and fish. You can get these served with hummus and imported Basmati rice pilaf. Vegetarians can choose a plate of four items such as hummus, moussaka, spinach, baba ghanuj, brown rice, tabbouleh, grape leaves, cheese pie, labneh, or falafel. Byblos' signature dessert that we devoured was the ashta (eggless custard wrapped in crunchy golden brown filo dough topped with orange blossom rosewater syrup and chopped pistachios). This dessert is a must. You will truly be delighted at Byblos.

MY NEW ORLEANS DINING JOURNAL

BYBLOS MARKET

Date & Time:_____Total Expense: _____

Companion(s):_____

Description of décor:_____

Directions to restaurant
and parking information:_____

_____

Service:_____

Favorite Food(s)/Wine(s):_____

_____

_____

_____

_____

My remarks and
impressions:_____

_____

_____

SAVE BUSINESS CARD OR RESTAURANT SOUVENIR HERE

BYBLOS MARKET

2020 Veterans Memorial Boulevard
Metairie, Louisiana 70002
(504) 837-9777

Metairie
Inexpensive to Moderate

Byblos Market is a wonderful Middle Eastern restaurant/grocery store. As you enter the store you will smell (and see) the gyros heating and twirling behind the counter. Immediately, you will want to order one of the gyros – but hold back and peruse what's inside the counter and on the menu. There are clean tables at which to sit and eat your chicken shawarma (fresh boneless chicken breast marinated overnight in lemon juice, garlic, and aromatic Lebanese spices broiled and thinly sliced served on Arabic pita with garlic sauce, lettuce, tomatoes and pickles). You can order at the counter and eat in, with such dishes as baba ghanuj Greek salad, tabbouleh, beef and lamb gyro, or falafel – that has fried fava and garbanzo beans mixed with herbs and spices, as well as tender rotisserie chicken.

For vegetarians, you may partake of the hummus (that brings you to another land), baba ghanuj, tabbouleh, grape leaves, rice pilaf, or salad. There are also some very sweet Middle Eastern desserts. Spend time in the market part of the store for authentic Middle Eastern items. This Lebanese market will be fascinating and flavorful, out-of-the-ordinary trip.

MY NEW ORLEANS DINING JOURNAL

CAFE ATCHAFALAYA

Date & Time:_____Total Expense: _____

Companion(s):_____

Description of décor:_____

Directions to restaurant
and parking information:_____

_____

Service:_____

Favorite Food(s)/Wine(s):_____

_____

_____

_____

_____

My remarks and
impressions:_____

_____

_____

_____

SAVE BUSINESS CARD OR RESTAURANT SOUVENIR HERE

CAFE' ATCHAFALAYA

901 Louisiana Avenue
New Orleans, Louisiana 70115
(504) 891-5271

Uptown
Inexpensive

Café Atchafalaya is a sure bet for catching some of the Southern local flavor here in New Orleans. Just blocks off St. Charles Avenue is a small, unpretentious down-home place to eat breakfast (on weekends), lunch, or dinner. You will feel welcome at any meal here.

For Northerners, grits and grillades at Café Atchafalaya are a good initiation to Southern indulgences. Fried green tomatoes, beef brisket, country fried steak, shrimp Creole, catfish pecan, Creole crabcakes with choron sauce, chicken and dumplings, black-eyed peas and chicken with ginger, and lime are all yummy. For pork chop lovers, experience Café Atchafalaya's thick stuffed chops. It also has daily specials listed on the chalkboard that will make you smack your lips. Café Atchafalaya is cash only, inexpensive, and easy to locate in its Uptown neighborhood. Must for dessert is the fruit cobblers or bread pudding. Early diners can take advantage of the earlybird dinner specials served between 5:30 p.m. and 7 p.m. Café Atchafalaya heralds Southern food with a gourmet flair. Here you'll get some Southern hospitality and good eatin.

MY NEW ORLEANS DINING JOURNAL

<u>CAFE GIOVANNI</u>

Date & Time:_____Total Expense: _____

Companion(s):_____

Description of décor:_____

Directions to restaurant
and parking information:_____

_____

Service:_____

Favorite Food(s)/Wine(s):_____

_____

_____

_____

_____

My remarks and
impressions:_____

_____

_____

_____

SAVE BUSINESS CARD OR RESTAURANT SOUVENIR HERE

CAFÉ GIOVANNI

117 Decatur Street
New Orleans, Louisiana 70130
(504) 529-2154

French Quarter   *Reservations Suggested*
Moderate to Expensive   *Open Evenings Only*

Chef/Owner Duke LoCicero has created a place where New World Italian Cuisine can flourish, grow, and be worshipped. This *dinner only* French Quarter Italian eatery is one of the few "French Quarter" restaurants to make our book. The reason is that it fit our criteria well. The food is not only excellent, served in an upscale, romantic ambiance, but has, for years, been adored by nearly every local we know. Café Giovanni is the type of place you'd most definitely dine with a special person. Preferably one who would enjoy the wine, opera-singing waiters, and luscious cuisine.

Chef LoCicero is a native, so he can't help but mix together the City's pervasive Italian and Creole traditions into something that is unique, rich in taste and ingredients, and an absolute pure delight. Not to be missed appetizers at Café Giovanni include Oysters Giovanni, Eggplant Locicero (breaded with jumbo crabmeat and shrimp with a Vodka dill cream sauce), and grilled portabella mushroom. Pastas include hunter's cannelloni, linguine pescatore, and others.

House Specialties include veal marsala, spicy seared pork filet (so unique, comes with crawfish, mirliton and tasso sauce, and a rosemary herbed pork demi-glace and risotto), grilled lamb chops, tournedos, veal Parmesan, and grilled shrimp dabney. Take it from locals who have enjoyed a fine dining experience for years, Café Giovanni provides great cuisine as well as perfect ambiance.

MY NEW ORLEANS DINING JOURNAL

<u>CHRISTIAN'S</u>

Date & Time:_____Total Expense: _____

Companion(s):_____

Description of décor:_____

Directions to restaurant
and parking information:_____

_____

Service:_____

Favorite Food(s)/Wine(s):_____

_____

_____

_____

_____

My remarks and
impressions:_____

_____

_____

_____

SAVE BUSINESS CARD OR RESTAURANT SOUVENIR HERE

CHRISTIAN'S

3835 Iberville Street
New Orleans, Louisiana 70119-5234
(504) 482-4924

Mid-City
Expensive   *Reservations Suggested*

If you'd ever had the desire to have a great meal while sitting in an old Church, this place is an answer to your prayers. Housed in an old Lutheran church built in 1914, Christian's began delighting New Orleans with its culinary genius back in 1977 and continues to please diners in a big way. Apart from the charming atmosphere replete with stained glass windows, cathedral ceilings, . . . Christian's serves up some devilishly delicious fare.

The perfect blending of Creole and classic French style dishes extend themselves into tantalizing poultry, meat, and seafood dishes. Try the Crawfish Carolyn as an appetizer (prepared in a spicy cream sauce with brandy and Parmesan cheese). Christian's Oysters Roland is another favorite as is the grilled duck salad. Favorite entrees include fish filet (meuniere or amandine), stuffed pork tenderloin (stuffed with andouille, artichoke, cornbread dressing and topped with apple brandy cream sauce, YES!), Shrimp Marigny, and any of the other surefire favorites that please both the palate and nearly all of the senses. Christian's offers a special sundown menu — complete with soup, salad, entree, dessert, coffee/tea, and glass of wine on Tuesday through Thursday. What an angelic way to start your evening! Dinner is served Tuesday through Saturday.

MY NEW ORLEANS DINING JOURNAL

<u>CLANCY'S</u>

Date & Time:_____Total Expense: _____

Companion(s):_____

Description of décor:_____

Directions to restaurant
and parking information:_____

_____

Service:_____

Favorite Food(s)/Wine(s):_____

_____

_____

_____

_____

My remarks and
impressions:_____

_____

_____

_____

SAVE BUSINESS CARD OR RESTAURANT SOUVENIR HERE

CLANCY'S

6100 Annunciation St.
New Orleans, Louisiana 70118-5709
(504) 895-1111

Uptown
Expensive   *Reservations Suggested*

Clancy's is located in an Uptown neighborhood that few tourists would find unless they ventured off the beaten track. It's a definite "see and be seen" favorite place of locals. Clancy's culinary popularity is well deserved and stems from its fabulous nouvelle Creole dishes and rare wines to its modest style which makes dining at Clancy's a relaxing and enjoyable experience focusing on good food and conversation.

Apart from the daily specials, dining at Clancy's gives you the opportunity to try some of the wines from its extensive list as well as a number of rare offerings by the glass. The bar at Clancy's is a good place to have a drink, mingle, and wait for a table to clear.

Some appetizer favorites include baked oysters with artichokes, kalamata olives and puffed pastry, and fried oysters with Brie. The sweetbreads appetizer is literally "out of this world." There is a seasonal salad offering as well as Clancy's chop salad and Boston salad with walnuts, hearts of palm and blue cheese. Pasta and risotto dishes such as risotto with lobster are offered in half or whole portions. Entrees that can't be missed include the veal chop with Marsala and mushrooms, filet mignon with Stilton and red wine demi-glace, paneed veal annunciation and smoked soft-shell crab with crabmeat. You won't regret dining here or having to wait for a table, we guarantee it.

MY NEW ORLEANS DINING JOURNAL

<u>CUVEE RESTAURANT</u>

Date & Time:_____Total Expense: _____

Companion(s):_____

Description of décor:_____

Directions to restaurant
and parking information:_____

_____

Service:_____

Favorite Food(s)/Wine(s):_____

_____

_____

_____

_____

My remarks and
impressions:_____

_____

_____

_____

SAVE BUSINESS CARD OR RESTAURANT SOUVENIR HERE

CUVÉE RESTAURANT

322 Magazine Street
New Orleans, Louisiana 70130
(504) 587-9001

Downtown
Expensive   *Reservations Suggested*

One of the absolute new favorite places to eat is Cuvée. The menu is creative and the wine and champagne offerings — outstanding. The talent and creativity of Chef Richard Starr has turned this place into one of New Orleans' best new places to dine. Cuvée's atmosphere is warm and upscale and lends itself well for assuring both favorable business meetings at lunchtime or a perfect place to take someone special for dinner.

For a prelude (appetizer) try the crispy mirliton and spicy shrimp Napoleon with tomato remoulade or the pan-seared scallops with sugar beets and fresh watercress. Salad offerings include a portobella confit with arugala and frisee, oven-cured tomatoes in bittersweet balsamic. Favorite entrees include the mustard and herb crusted salmon filet on lump crabmeat and Brie orzo and the filet of beef on truffle-creamed leeks-spinach-potatoes, sugar cane-smoked duck breast with Roquefort-pecan risotto and *foie gras*. The lunch menu has additional items not included on the dinner menu such as pan roasted rainbow trout, herb-roasted half chicken, smoked beef short ribs, and seafood bouillabaisse.

MY NEW ORLEANS DINING JOURNAL

<u>DEANIE'S SEAFOOD</u>

Date & Time:_____Total Expense: _____

Companion(s):_____

Description of décor:_____

Directions to restaurant
and parking information:_____

_____

Service:_____

Favorite Food(s)/Wine(s):_____

_____

_____

_____

_____

My remarks and
impressions:_____

_____

_____

_____

SAVE BUSINESS CARD OR RESTAURANT SOUVENIR HERE

DEANIE'S SEAFOOD RESTAURANT

1713 Lake Avenue   841 Iberbille Street
Metairie, LA 70005   New Orleans, LA 70112
(504) 831-4141

Bucktown
Moderate

Deanie's spells seafood in all caps. It should. For years it has been nestled in the middle of many seafood vendors in Bucktown near Lake Pontchartrain. This is one of the areas where fisherman bring their catch fresh off the boats to sell. Deanie's has its own store that sells all the popular food that locals love like fresh fish, boiled seafood like crawfish, crabs, shrimp, and oysters, potato salad, and more.

The atmosphere at Deanie's is casual; full of local families and people committed to getting more for their money. So, tuck your napkin in your shirt and get ready to put your fingers into a large platter of boiled crawfish or shrimp! Should you try the Giant Seafood Platter, you will share it with at least one or two other people in your group. Also try the fried artichoke hearts, fried soft-shell crabs, seafood gumbo, fried onion rings, crab claws, crabmeat au gratin, fried oysters, broiled or stuffed flounder or BBQ shrimp. Whatever you order will satisfy your appetite not only at the time, but also perhaps for a few days! The service is good and the price is right (you won't complain). Locals like to meet their families after work at Deanie's for a satisfying and fulfilling meal.

MY NEW ORLEANS DINING JOURNAL
<u>DICK & JENNY'S</u>

Date & Time:_____Total Expense: _____

Companion(s):_____

Description of décor:_____

Directions to restaurant
and parking information:_____

_____

Service:_____

Favorite Food(s)/Wine(s):_____

_____

_____

_____

_____

My remarks and
impressions:_____

_____

_____

_____

SAVE BUSINESS CARD OR RESTAURANT SOUVENIR HERE

DICK & JENNY'S

4501 Tchoupitoulas Street
New Orleans, Louisiana 70115
(504) 894-9880

Uptown
Moderate to Expensive

Dick & Jenny's is probably one of the most creative local restaurants in the City. When I first went to Dick & Jenny's there was a long wait (over and hour) with our close friends, Pat and Ray. Since there are no reservations taken at Dick & Jenny's — there probably will be a wait. However, the wait is definitely worth it. We sat in the patio in the back of the restaurant and enjoyed chatting and meeting old friends; I was surprised to see so many of my local friends in the patio too.

What makes Dick & Jenny's inventive is its menu; imaginative and creative — it also changes every few months. Dick & Jenny's opens for dinner Tuesday through Saturday. Duck is a very popular item on the menu. Their 2001 summer menu offered grilled duck breast salad with apples, pears, pecans, green beans, dried cherries, and Gorgonzola. Mouth watering is the bronzed pork tenderloin stuffed with spinach, goat cheese and pinenuts over smoked corn grits with tomato balsamic vinaigrette, and seafood bouillabaisse (mussels, calamari, shrimp, crab and gulf fish in a saffron fish stew with rouille). As you can see, the menu at Dick & Jenny's is exceptional. Dick & Jenny's is one true catch in the sea of restaurants. Your dining experience and evening will be one that you will want to figuratively hang on your mantle for everyone to see.

MY NEW ORLEANS DINING JOURNAL

<u>DOOKY CHASE</u>

Date & Time:_____Total Expense: _____

Companion(s):_____

Description of décor:_____

Directions to restaurant
and parking information:_____

_____

Service:_____

Favorite Food(s)/Wine(s):_____

_____

_____

_____

_____

My remarks and
impressions:_____

_____

_____

_____

SAVE BUSINESS CARD OR RESTAURANT SOUVENIR HERE

DOOKY CHASE

2301 Orleans Avenue
New Orleans, Louisiana 70119-5025
(504) 821-0600

Mid-City
Moderate

Dooky Chase is one of New Orleans most established Creole dining landmarks. For many years now, Dooky Chase has been a favorite meeting and dining place for local politicians and community leaders alike. The dining area is comfortable and glamorous and a celebration of local life. Local African-American artists adorn the walls with their colorful artwork and the windows have stained-glass panels depicting life in New Orleans. Restaurant owner, Leah Chase, is a well-known community leader as well as successful chef who began her career with Dooky Chase some 54 years ago when she was hired to work in her mother-in-law's restaurant.

If you're serious about having traditional Creole and soul food dishes in a city that does it better than anywhere else, Dooky Chase is the place to go. Some local favorites at Dooky Chase include the Shrimp Dooky, fried chicken (a lot of locals I know say that this is the only fried chicken in town), shrimp clemenceau (I love garlic, so this is a real delight – it is mixed with potatoes, onions and peas in butter), veal grilliades with jambalaya, paneed veal, and gumbo. If you want to try a smacking of lunchtime delights, come for the buffet that is served daily beginning at 11 a.m. Some of New Orleans' best chefs have taken their cues from Dooky Chase. Don't forget dessert . . . bread pudding to die for!

MY NEW ORLEANS DINING JOURNAL

<u>DRAGO'S</u>

Date & Time:_____Total Expense: _____

Companion(s):_____

Description of décor:_____

Directions to restaurant
and parking information:_____

_____

Service:_____

Favorite Food(s)/Wine(s):_____

_____

_____

_____

_____

My remarks and
impressions:_____

_____

_____

_____

SAVE BUSINESS CARD OR RESTAURANT SOUVENIR HERE

DRAGO'S

3232 N. Arnoult Road
Metairie, Louisiana 70002
(504) 888-9254

Metairie
Moderate

Drago's is the premier place for seafood in the sub-urbs. Specifically, it is famous for its chargrilled oysters. Our favorite thing to do at Drago's is to eat/drink at the bar where we can watch the oysters as they are shucked and then charbroiled in their shells on an open grill. As we eat, we also enjoy the aroma of the garlic, butter, and cheese placed on each oyster as they are grilled. Needless to say, the oysters melt in your mouth; some folks come from as far as 50 miles away regularly just for this one dish – Drago's original chargrilled oysters (only $11.95 for a dozen). The service is professional and the restaurant is upbeat and happy.

The Owners — the Cvitanovich family, are usually around (mostly Klara and Tommy) – and you can see lovely pictures they proudly display of their children and grand-children on the bar. Drago's is known for seafood and includes in its menu gulf shrimp, trout, and red snapper (fried to golden perfection). Other delightful items include oyster spinach soup, lobster salad, mesquite-grilled shrimp salad, lobster Marco (a whole lobster stuffed with fresh sautéed shrimp and mushrooms in a cream sauce over angel hair pasta), stuffed whole Maine lobster (filled with fresh crabmeat and shrimp dressing), bayou duck (strips of roasted duck, shrimp, and crabmeat cooked with a white cream sauce and stuffed in a bread bowl), veal Alfredo, and stuffed crab. Because of Drago's popularity, you may want to arrive early or be prepared to wait, especially if it is a Friday or Saturday night.

MY NEW ORLEANS DINING JOURNAL

FEELINGS CAFE D'AUNOY

Date & Time:_____Total Expense: _____

Companion(s):_____

Description of décor:_____

Directions to restaurant
and parking information:_____

_____

Service:_____

Favorite Food(s)/Wine(s):_____

_____

_____

_____

_____

My remarks and
impressions:_____

_____

_____

_____

SAVE BUSINESS CARD OR RESTAURANT SOUVENIR HERE

FEELINGS CAFÉ D'AUNOY

2600 Chartres Street
New Orleans, Louisiana 70117-7312
(504) 945-2222

Faubourg Marigny
Moderate   *Reservations Suggested*

Locals love to go to Feelings Café. It's a true New Orleans landmark housed in one of the City's oldest neighborhoods. The building is full of history and provides an intimate and interesting place to dine that includes three dining areas — an atmospheric main dining room, a sweet-as-pie courtyard, and a balcony with tables for two along side of the slave quarters that overlook the courtyard. The bar is narrow, but lively, and often has a pianist playing wonderful tunes that fill the air. Additionally, upstairs has two larger dining rooms for great private functions.

The service at Feelings Café is very good and the wait staff is not only knowledgeable about the dishes and wines served, but enthusiastic to make recommendations that are sure pleasers. Some of the tried and fantastically true favorites at Feelings are the special red snapper served over spinach cooked with Pernod, the Bleu cheese steak (with sautéed mushrooms, new potatoes, and a vegetable), and the Duck Bigarde [the best duck I have ever eaten] cooked crispy and glazed with a semi-sweet orange sauce made with Gran Marnier and served on a bed of flavorful pecan rice. The seafood-baked eggplant is a true original and has locals coming back year after year.

For dessert, there are plentiful offerings, including a unique flan (not on the menu but available) that is absolutely unforgettable. Feelings Café is a great place to indulge in both great food and atmosphere of old New Orleans.

MY NEW ORLEANS DINING JOURNAL

<u>FIVE HAPPINESS</u>

Date & Time:_____Total Expense: _____

Companion(s):_____

Description of décor:_____

Directions to restaurant
and parking information:_____

_____

Service:_____

Favorite Food(s)/Wine(s):_____

_____

_____

_____

_____

My remarks and
impressions:_____

_____

_____

_____

SAVE BUSINESS CARD OR RESTAURANT SOUVENIR HERE

FIVE HAPPINESS

3605 S. Carrollton Ave.
New Orleans, Louisiana 70118-4509
(504) 482-3935

Mid-City
Inexpensive to Moderate

Of all the Chinese places around New Orleans, Five Happiness is the one that always keeps locals coming back. The restaurant is large, comfortable, and the food, a delight. Not only is it creative beyond what you would find in many other restaurants, locals who've frequented Five Happiness during its 20 years of existence marvel at the consistency in both quality and service.

The hot and sour soup, shrimp with sizzling rice soup, and the chicken with corn soup are all excellent. House specialties include sizzling go-ba, pecan shrimp with sesame seeds, sizzling scallops, savory crispy soft-shell crab, house baked duck, and a number of other seafood, pork, beef, and poultry dishes. Five Happiness has won a number of awards, including "Best Chinese Restaurant" by *New Orleans Magazine* and *Gambit* among others. I find this a good place to go with my entire family, including in-laws. We sit at the big round table for 8-10 persons, spin the food around, and sample a little of everyone's order. Another good point about this place is that it's nearly always open, even on holidays. Five Happiness . . . where Chinese and New Orleans cuisine fuses.

MY NEW ORLEANS DINING JOURNAL

<u>FURY'S RESTAURANT</u>

Date & Time:_____Total Expense: _____

Companion(s):_____

Description of décor:_____

Directions to restaurant
and parking information:_____

_____

Service:_____

Favorite Food(s)/Wine(s):_____

_____

_____

_____

_____

My remarks and
impressions:_____

_____

_____

_____

SAVE BUSINESS CARD OR RESTAURANT SOUVENIR HERE

FURY'S RESTAURANT

724 Martin Behrman Avenue
Metairie, Louisiana 70005
(504) 834-5646

Metairie
Moderate

Nestled on Martin Behrman Avenue in Metairie, Fury's is hardly noticeable from outside. Its interior is not particularly outstanding or rememberable either. This family-owned restaurant has been in business since 1982 and boasts a dedicated following who swear by its "made-to-order" menu. Patrons at Fury's don't mind the wait and many even call ahead and place their orders when time is an issue. Fury's has daily specials like on Monday's — red beans & rice (would it be a New Orleans restaurant without it?). Also, stuffed peppers are on the menu everyday and taste just like mama used to make.

If you're in the mood to eat and eat a lot (and have the time), Fury's won't disappoint you. Some of the favorites include crabmeat au gratin and veal Metairie (served with lump crabmeat and shrimp over angel hair pasta). The onion rings are unlike any other; the secret is in the batter. The veal Parmesan is delicious. I really appreciated the sauce with angel hair pasta — it has a distinctive home-made flavor and is not overly done. At Fury's, it's like you have just ordered pasta while in Italy! For seafood lovers, there are a number of specials that include shrimp, soft-shell crab almondine, fish in oyster sauce, and a seafood combination. If you're in Metairie and feel like eating like a native, try Fury's . . . the local's around love it.

MY NEW ORLEANS DINING JOURNAL

<u>GABRIELLE</u>

Date & Time:_____Total Expense: _____

Companion(s):_____

Description of décor:_____

Directions to restaurant
and parking information:_____

_____

Service:_____

Favorite Food(s)/Wine(s):_____

_____

_____

_____

_____

My remarks and
impressions:_____

_____

_____

_____

SAVE BUSINESS CARD OR RESTAURANT SOUVENIR HERE

GABRIELLE

3201 Esplanade Avenue
New Orleans, Louisiana 70119-3129
(504) 948-6233

Mid-City
Moderate to Expensive   *Reservations Suggested*

Sitting right on the lush Esplanade Avenue is a small and uniquely-shaped restaurant known and loved by locals named Gabrielle. Gabrielle is a romantic place with a diverse menu that is always delicious and interesting. There is real innovation here by the owner/chef couple, Greg and Mary Sonnier, and they make dining at Gabrielle a real pleasure. The food styling is best described (in my mind) as inventive Creole. The menu changes weekly and locals always come back to try the next new dish out of the kitchen. The service is personable and friendly — Gabrielle's owners are making sure it stays that way.

Some favorites at Gabrielle are the pan-roasted T-bone steak served in Creole mustard, grilled andouille sausages that comes with fruit sauce for dipping, roasted duck, and a variety of seafood entrees. There is a prix fixe menu also and a wine list that includes a repertoire of good complimentary offerings. For dessert, Mary Sonnier whips up some mean sorbets, fresh fruit cobblers, apple bread pudding, and ice cream. Since Gabrielle is a small restaurant and very popular, it is always best to make reservations. To experience the talents of one of New Orleans most innovative chef's, Gabrielle is highly recommended – the atmosphere is charming and bistro-like and the food is nothing short of genius.

MY NEW ORLEANS DINING JOURNAL

<u>GAUTREAU'S RESTAURANT</u>

Date & Time:_____Total Expense: _____

Companion(s):_____

Description of décor:_____

Directions to restaurant
and parking information:_____

_____

Service:_____

Favorite Food(s)/Wine(s):_____

_____

_____

_____

_____

My remarks and
impressions:_____

_____

_____

_____

SAVE BUSINESS CARD OR RESTAURANT SOUVENIR HERE

GAUTREAU'S RESTAURANT

1728 Soniat Street
New Orleans, Louisiana 70115-4919
(504) 899-7397

Uptown
Moderate to Expensive   *Reservations Suggested*

This small renowned neighborhood restaurant lies in, of all things, a former pharmacy just a couple of blocks off of St. Charles Avenue. The atmosphere is beaming with New Orleans flair set in a venue that is quaint and stylish. Maintaining the historical property structure, the owners have turned antique apothecary cases into stunning wall-to-wall wine cabinets. Named after Madame Pierre Gautreau, the woman in John Singer Sargeant's portrait of Madame X, the former owner/relative dedicated the restaurant name after the 19th Century Parisian belle.

Talented Chef, Brent Bond, takes Gautreau's into the 21st Century with a menu that is all about quality, not quantity. Every six weeks, the menu reinvents itself and the dazzle remains. Open for dinner only, Gautreau's is meant for the serious diner. In-season game dishes are included on the menu and dishes such as rack of lamb, roast duck, fish, and chicken are sure pleasers. Desserts seem to be luscious affairs also. Diners at Gautreau's are mostly dressed up and reservations are a must. Gautreau's is New Orleans food at its best. You'll see what we in New Orleans mean when we talk about great cuisine.

MY NEW ORLEANS DINING JOURNAL

<u>GENGHIS KHAN</u>

Date & Time:_____Total Expense: _____

Companion(s):_____

Description of décor:_____

Directions to restaurant
and parking information:_____

_____

Service:_____

Favorite Food(s)/Wine(s):_____

_____

_____

_____

_____

My remarks and
impressions:_____

_____

_____

_____

SAVE BUSINESS CARD OR RESTAURANT SOUVENIR HERE

GENGHIS KHAN

201 Baronne Street
New Orleans, Louisiana 70112
(504) 299-9009

Downtown
Moderate

Genghis Khan is unique in New Orleans and can be best described as a musical Korean restaurant. Okay, I know that sounds funny but it's true. Owner/classical violinist, Henry Lee (formerly with the New Orleans symphony), has operated Genghis Kahn for over twenty years – and his practice has paid off. Since he walks and plays his violin too, the question arises: "Do you go for the food or the music?" We'll let you decide and if you are a musician and like to perform on the spot, this also is for you. The waiters, for the most part, are well-trained, aspiring or former opera singers and are good ones at that. They take your order as a recitative then begin an aria (even when you haven't asked). A prominent attorney dining is likely to interrupt his meal, stand up and sing an Irish ballad like *O'Danny Boy* with piano accompaniment.

Though the singing is impromptu, the food is not. The Korean food is good and has an American slant. The restaurant's forte is the garlic shrimp, beef bulgoki (thinly sliced beef) as well as the whole fried fish. Eating (or even singing) at Genghis Khan will be an enjoyable experience (unless you can't sing) that you may never forget. Genghis Khan is not only about the good food, but a great place to try out your *Caro Mio Ben*.

MY NEW ORLEANS DINING JOURNAL

IRENE'S CUISINE

Date & Time:_____Total Expense: _____

Companion(s):_____

Description of décor:_____

Directions to restaurant
and parking information:_____

_____

Service:_____

Favorite Food(s)/Wine(s):_____

_____

_____

_____

_____

My remarks and
impressions:_____

_____

_____

_____

SAVE BUSINESS CARD OR RESTAURANT SOUVENIR HERE

IRENE'S CUISINE

539 Saint Philip Street
New Orleans, Louisiana 70116
(504) 529-8811

French Quarter
Moderate

Hugely popular with locals, Irene's Cuisine is a busy, high-energy place where the wait for a table begins promptly upon its opening around 5:30 p.m. Irene Di Pietro has created a French Quarter trattoria where the cuisine is largely Sicilian with some Creole influence. The "no reservations" policy (oddly) adds to the fun of the place as locals crowd in with their wine glasses, visit, while all the while, piano music fills the background air. With an atmosphere that's both colorful and romantic, plus some dishes that are literally to die for, Irene's remains one of the top spots in New Orleans.

While the food here is consistently good and oftentimes just unmistakably "superb," there are a number of dishes that are so good that locals admit that they've gotten stuck on them. Among the favorites — the roasted chicken with rosemary and olive oil, oysters Irene, sautéed soft-shell crab, the grilled red snapper with shrimp and peppers, and any of the veal dishes. Local friends of mine from Italy adore the food here. (It's a rare occasion and good sign when Italians approve of any restaurant outside of Italy — as do people all around the City). There are a good number of wines from Italy and great coffee to chaperone your dessert (Tiramisu rules!). Advice for Irene's – always get there early — but if there is a bit of a wait, don't fret, it'll be worth it. Buon Appetito!

MY NEW ORLEANS DINING JOURNAL

<u>JACQUES-IMO CAFE</u>

Date & Time:_____Total Expense: _____

Companion(s):_____

Description of décor:_____

Directions to restaurant
and parking information:_____

_____

Service:_____

Favorite Food(s)/Wine(s):_____

_____

_____

_____

_____

My remarks and
impressions:_____

_____

_____

_____

SAVE BUSINESS CARD OR RESTAURANT SOUVENIR HERE

JACQUES-IMO CAFÉ

8324 Oak Street
New Orleans, Louisiana 70118-2044
(504) 861-0886

Uptown
Expensive

This funky little café is worth visiting just for the fact that it is one of the absolute favorite restaurants of many of the local chefs. The atmosphere is casual, the style, a little offbeat (to say the least), and the wait for a table (six or more in your party get reservations only) nearly always something to expect. However, the experience of eating at Jacques-Imo's is worth the wait. Open for dinner only, there is an extensive wine list to compliment whatever you may order.

Some of the special creations include appetizers like shrimp and alligator sausage cheesecake, oyster Brie soup with champagne, and fried soft-shell crab almondine. You will find a diverse and extensive number of entrees and all include a house salad and your choice of two vegetables. Favorites include blackened loin of lamb with Dijon mango cream sauce, paneed rabbit with an oyster tasso pasta, New Orleans style BBQ shrimp, and mushroom stuffed grilled salmon. Exciting sauces compliment just about every meat, seafood, or pasta dish you can imagine. Some that stand out for me are the oyster tasso hollandaise, Oriental black bean and ginger sauce, and pistachio sauce and asparagus that covers the grilled amberjack! Heavenly! The bar is cute and a fun place to hang out while waiting for a table or just to have a drink.

MY NEW ORLEANS DINING JOURNAL

<u>JAMILIA'S CAFE</u>

Date & Time:_____Total Expense: _____

Companion(s):_____

Description of décor:_____

Directions to restaurant
and parking information:_____

_____

Service:_____

Favorite Food(s)/Wine(s):_____

_____

_____

_____

_____

My remarks and
impressions:_____

_____

_____

_____

SAVE BUSINESS CARD OR RESTAURANT SOUVENIR HERE

JAMILIA'S CAFÉ

7808 Maple Street
New Orleans, Louisiana 70118
(504) 866-4366

Uptown
Moderate

For authentic North African/Tunisian cuisine served in a friendly and relaxed manner, locals love Jamilia's Café's casual atmosphere. Family owned and operated, Jamila's serves up its star cuisine with homemade flair and freshness. The dishes are traditional fare and entree portions are ample.

Many of the dishes come served with couscous. The sauces and stews simmer with exotic flavors and spices. The dining space is quaint and atmospheric and the service is attentive (the owner is usually serving and interested in knowing just how much you enjoyed the meal). Interesting appetizers include the brik aux crevettes (filo dough stuffed with shrimp, potatoes, parsley and onions), ojja merguex (homemade lamb sausage), Jamila's Chorba (whole-wheat fish soup with capers and lemon), Jamila's crawfish, zucchini and spinach bisque, and a whole array of fresh salads.

Entrees include petite filet, calamari maison (squid stuffed with shrimp), mechoui en brochettes (grilled lamb skewers served with couscous and vegetables), and Tunisian signature dishes (including couscous either vegetarian, au poulet, au poisson, a l'agneau, and royal). For dessert, try Jamila's pastries or the crème brulee. Enjoy the food, the atmosphere, and the hospitality — it's the reason Jamila's Café is a local favorite. Hear a classical guitarist on Friday or go Saturday night for belly dancer night!

MY NEW ORLEANS DINING JOURNAL

<u>KATIE'S</u>

Date & Time:_____Total Expense: _____

Companion(s):_____

Description of décor:_____

Directions to restaurant
and parking information:_____

_____

Service:_____

Favorite Food(s)/Wine(s):_____

_____

_____

_____

_____

My remarks and
impressions:_____

_____

_____

_____

SAVE BUSINESS CARD OR RESTAURANT SOUVENIR HERE

KATIE'S

3701 Iberville Street
New Orleans, Louisiana 70119-5232
(504) 488-6582

Mid-City
Inexpensive

Since 1984, Katie's has been a real Mid-City neighborhood favorite. It has a very relaxed atmosphere, attentive staff, and local flavor. Katie's is not a large restaurant inside, but friendly. New Orleanians find all their favorite foods here – muffalettas, seafood gumbo, stuffed crabs, softshell crabs, BBQ shrimp, fried catfish (thin-cut, how else?), chicken Marsala and angel hair pasta, eggplant Parmesan and angel hair marinara, and stuffed shrimp dinner.

Katie's has over 20 different types of sandwiches from grilled cheese to oyster po-boy sandwiches ranging from $3.95 to $8.95. The prices are right and the food really enjoyable. You may even want to try the grilled calf's liver and onions or the pork chops ($7.95). Katie's also has grilled fresh fish, filet mignon, bronzed catfish, and even potato po-boy sandwiches. For those that want beer or wine, there is a good selection and also included is "New Orleans Original" Dixie Beer. (Hey, at one time we all drank Dixie.) In any event, Katie's is a great place if you want good food in a casual setting. A fried oyster po-boy from Katie's would really make your day.

MY NEW ORLEANS DINING JOURNAL

<u>KELSEY'S RESTAURANT</u>

Date & Time:_____Total Expense: _____

Companion(s):_____

Description of décor:_____

Directions to restaurant
and parking information:_____

_____

Service:_____

Favorite Food(s)/Wine(s):_____

_____

_____

_____

_____

My remarks and
impressions:_____

_____

_____

_____

SAVE BUSINESS CARD OR RESTAURANT SOUVENIR HERE

KELSEY'S RESTAURANT

3923 Magazine Street
New Orleans, Louisiana 70115
(504) 897-6722

Uptown
Moderate to Expensive

Having received numerous local and national reviews (including Wine Spectator's Award of Excellence 2002), Kelsey's remains a New Orleans gem. Located on Magazine Street, just two miles from the CBD, Chef Tait Guthrie serves up a number of creative influences. By far one of our favorites, Kelsey's has a casual, yet elegant atmosphere where you can take your time and share a bottle of wine or two at dinner.

Kelsey's focus is on fresh seafood, veal, beef, and pasta dishes. For an appetizer, try Danny's grilled oysters (grilled in its shell) with Stilton cheese, fresh garlic and herbs, or the crab and fried green tomato Napoleon. As a salad, try Kelsey's fresh arugula and watermelon with raspberry balsamic and spiced walnuts, or the Caesar salad with wilted radicchio, shaved Parmesan cheese with herbed crostini topped with avocado mousse. Entrées include Michal's pan-seared Airline chicken breast over white bean and baby spinach ragout with a roasted red pepper coulis, the lemongrass-crusted salmon in a sweet ginger jus over basmati rice served with pickled cucumber salad, or the double cut pork chop stuffed with cornbread pecan stuffing glazed with a maple jus - all are mouthwatering!

For dessert, try the white chocolate mousse with Galliano infused strawberries and basil chiffonade, café au lait crème brulee, or the flourless chocolate ganach tort with raspberry coulis. Indulge yourself at Kelsey's; Kelsey's won't disappoint.

MY NEW ORLEANS DINING JOURNAL

LA CREPE NANOU

Date & Time:_____Total Expense: _____

Companion(s):_____

Description of décor:_____

Directions to restaurant
and parking information:_____

_____

Service:_____

Favorite Food(s)/Wine(s):_____

_____

_____

_____

_____

My remarks and
impressions:_____

_____

_____

_____

SAVE BUSINESS CARD OR RESTAURANT SOUVENIR HERE

LA CREPE NANOU

1410 Robert Street
New Orleans, Louisiana 70115
(504) 899-2670

Uptown
Moderate

Uptown New Orleanians have been enjoying a little bit of Paris at La Crepe Nanou for 18 years now. With consistency in cuisine and atmosphere, this charming bistro is open for dinner only and is the perfect place for a romantic evening. The menu at La Crepe Nanou includes many classic French dishes, ones you'd expect to find in any bistro in France. And though the name of the restaurant makes you think its all about crepes (and there are a number of great ones) there's a lot more to get excited about.

Some favorite dishes at La Crepe Nanou include Les Moules Marinieres (mussels steamed in garlic, cream, and white wine), Les Cotelletes d'Agneau (lamb chops with cognac sauce), La Fondue, "L'Assiete de Pates et Fromages" (plate with mixed pate and cheese), Les Crepes (the crabmeat and spinach crepe is delicious), any of the fish dishes (especially the salmon) and finally, Les Bonnes Crepes — a literal plethora of dessert crepes. The "Crepe Nanou" is the signature favorite dessert crepe with vanilla, chocolate, and coffee ice cream topped with almonds and chocolate sauce. The wine list is quite nice and includes California, Italian, and French wines. If you like French food and atmosphere, we are sure you will not be disappointed by La Crepe Nanou. Vive La France and remember, La Crepe Nanou does not take reservations.

MY NEW ORLEANS DINING JOURNAL

LE PARVENU RESTAURANT

Date & Time:_____Total Expense: _____

Companion(s):_____

Description of décor:_____

Directions to restaurant
and parking information:_____

_____

Service:_____

Favorite Food(s)/Wine(s):_____

_____

_____

_____

_____

My remarks and
impressions:_____

_____

_____

_____

SAVE BUSINESS CARD OR RESTAURANT SOUVENIR HERE

LE PARVENU RESTAURANT

509 Williams Boulevard
Kenner, Louisiana 70062
(504) 471-0534

Kenner
Moderate to Expensive

As restaurants go, Le Parvenu is not terribly old –
established in 1996, however, the chef, Dennis Hutley has
plenty of experience. Le Parvenu is set in a restored 50-year
old house fronted with a white picket fence near the
Mississippi River in the Historic District of Rivertown (about
20 minutes from downtown New Orleans). You certainly
will want to take a stroll in this historic area before or after
dining.

Le Parvenu credits itself as having innovative
American Creole cuisine that serves lunch and dinner
Tuesday through Saturday and also a Sunday brunch.
What I find amazing is that this very upscale but moderate-
ly priced restaurant has a great children's menu with items
such as sautéed shrimp and fettuccini, grilled petit filet with
vegetables and potatoes, and paneed veal with fettuccini,
or a simple grilled cheese sandwich. (I like restaurants that
forgo chicken tenders for my children.) This is a very popular place for parties and rehearsal dinners because of the
historic location and quaint look of this cottage.

The lunch entrees are spectacular – seafood crepes,
paneed pork loin with "Jezebel" salsa, fillet of snapper or
boiled beef brisket with carrots and potatoes. On the dinner
menu you may order what is called "And Den Sum" – a four
course sampler of Le Parvenu's menu (for only $29). Le
Parvenu would also be a great place to go for Sunday
brunch. I can see why Le Parvenu was rated top ten in New
Orleans by 1999 *Zagat Survey*. Hats off to Chef Dennis!

MY NEW ORLEANS DINING JOURNAL

LIUZZA'S RESTAURANT & BAR

Date & Time:_____Total Expense: _____

Companion(s):_____

Description of décor:_____

Directions to restaurant
and parking information:_____

_____

Service:_____

Favorite Food(s)/Wine(s):_____

_____

_____

_____

_____

My remarks and
impressions:_____

_____

_____

_____

SAVE BUSINESS CARD OR RESTAURANT SOUVENIR HERE

LIUZZA'S RESTAURANT & BAR

3636 Bienville Street
New Orleans, Louisiana 70119
(504) 482-9120

Mid-City
Inexpensive

Liuzza's is an authentic New Orleans neighborhood favorite that's been around for many generations. The atmosphere is casual and lively, the prices are good and the food is tasty. Here you will see New Orleans families and regulars eating to their hearts delight (hey, that's just what we like to do here, okay). There's a bar at the entrance and the dining room is limited in space. The activity and bustle of the wait staff and the laughter of customers fills the dining area. If you haven't been to any of the New Orleans neighborhood restaurants, this is about as real as it gets.

A specialty of Liuzza's is the large frozen beer mugs that just about everyone seems to be enjoying. The special sandwich here is the "Frenchuletta" – Liuzza's version of the "muffelatta" served with grilled meats on French bread and topped with Michael's homemade olive salad. The seafood dishes are plentiful and come with side orders. The catfish topped with sautéed shrimp, white wine and butter, is great. The homemade fries are a big hit as is the roast beef po-boy with brown gravy, and pasta dishes have a real homemade, Italian taste. It's hard not to enjoy a meal here and feel like you're getting your money's worth. You'll feel like a real local at Liuzza's and you will understand what it means to be from New Orleans.

MY NEW ORLEANS DINING JOURNAL

<u>MANDICH RESTAURANT</u>

Date & Time:_____Total Expense: _____

Companion(s):_____

Description of décor:_____

Directions to restaurant
and parking information:_____

_____

Service:_____

Favorite Food(s)/Wine(s):_____

_____

_____

_____

_____

My remarks and
impressions:_____

_____

_____

_____

SAVE BUSINESS CARD OR RESTAURANT SOUVENIR HERE

MANDICH RESTAURANT

3200 St. Claude Avenue
New Orleans, Louisiana 70117
(504) 947-9553

Bywater
Expensive

Anyone in New Orleans who knows anything about good food is a regular customer of Mandich Restaurant. Lloyd and Joel English have found the secret to preparing consistently great-tasting seafood. As you walk in from a 9th Ward neighborhood that is definitely blue-collar, you may find Lloyd at the bar preparing a good old fashion. Joel (Lloyd's lovely wife) is in the kitchen checking on the roasted pork loin with candied yams or the sweet potato duck with crab cake.

They have it down – 54 years and still going strong. Mandich Restaurant is open for lunch and dinner. Lunch at Mandich's is a popular place for the downtown crowd. At lunch (Tuesday through Friday) you may try the bordelaise oysters (crisp on the half shell with (of course) garlic, broiled calf's liver with smothered onions, hot roast beef poor boy sandwich, grilled yellow fin tuna topped with "Cajun popcorn" (deep-fried crawfish tails with mild remoulade sauce), or the combination lunch (thin and crisp baby veal as well as the crabmeat au gratin with pasta, potato, or vegetable).

Dinner (Friday and Saturday) gets even better with the crab delight — fried soft-shell crab (bordelaise sauce optional) as well as crabmeat Bienville, eggplant and veal Parmesan, or sweet potato duck. One of my favorite tastes at Mandich's is their Louisiana sweet potatoes. Anything you order at Mandich's will be a feast for your taste buds. You'll really enjoy going to Mandich's — a very local, down-home, non-touristy sanctuary of great eating.

MY NEW ORLEANS DINING JOURNAL

__MANDINA'S RESTAURANT__

Date & Time:_____Total Expense: _____

Companion(s):_____

Description of décor:_____

Directions to restaurant
and parking information:_____

_____

Service:_____

Favorite Food(s)/Wine(s):_____

_____

_____

_____

_____

My remarks and
impressions:_____

_____

_____

_____

SAVE BUSINESS CARD OR RESTAURANT SOUVENIR HERE

MANDINA'S RESTAURANT

3800 Canal Street
New Orleans, Louisiana 70119-6037
(504) 482-9179

Mid-City
Inexpensive to Moderate

Right along the Canal Street bus line is one of New Orleans' oldest established neighborhood restaurants . . . Mandina's. Here, down home is the word. Experience real New Orleans cuisine in a friendly, casual neighborhood establishment at moderate prices. There's a different special each day of the week and the portions will not disappoint you.

Recommended is the turtle soup, crab claws, shrimp étouffée, soft-shell crab almondine, shrimp remoulade, red beans and rice, meatballs and spaghetti, and fried oysters po-boy. Basically, Mandina's serves up eats that are Italian and Creole-styled. Some of the specials this week are stuffed bell peppers, trout meuniere, ribeye steak and Creole catfish. The atmosphere is lively and familiar and totally New Orleans. This is a great place for lunch and the dress is always casual. This is one of Donald's (Debby's husband) favorite places to go to meet friends and eat. A lot of business people come here for lunch to enjoy a fried shrimp fix. Mandina's has proven itself to be reliably consistent in serving tasty local-spun delights — one of the best secrets kept by New Orleans' locals.

MY NEW ORLEANS DINING JOURNAL

<u>MAT & NADDIE'S CAFE</u>

Date & Time:_____Total Expense: _____

Companion(s):_____

Description of décor:_____

Directions to restaurant
and parking information:_____

_____

Service:_____

Favorite Food(s)/Wine(s):_____

_____

_____

_____

_____

My remarks and
impressions:_____

_____

_____

_____

SAVE BUSINESS CARD OR RESTAURANT SOUVENIR HERE

MAT & NADDIE'S CAFE

937 Leonidas Street
New Orleans, Louisiana 70113
(504) 861-9600

Uptown
Moderate to Expensive

Nestled Uptown near the Mississippi River and the railroad tracks is just the type of restaurant that Native New Orleanians like to keep to themselves. Mat & Naddie's is housed in a quaint Creole cottage with large windows, and artwork by local artists on the wall. Only in New Orleans can you find an oyster Rockefeller Pizza as a starter to your meal. The chef re-creates local dishes with South East Asian flair.

Recommended at Mat & Naddie's are the filet mignon with pepper and butter with rosemary, new potatoes, caramelized onions and balsamic reduction, the rack of lamb, and the very popular grilled oysters. Locals, Dimitri and Ashley, really like the braised Belgian endive salad with candied pecan mignonette and Stilton cheese with the smoked Cornish game (served with creamy sage and Romano grits and gravy). You may also like to try the popular Vietnamese spring rolls, Japanese seaweed salad, Thai beef salad, BBQ pork loin sandwich, or the crawfish cakes. Venison and other less common meats are done here and done very well. The Salmon is cooked just right and a favorite of many locals. For dessert, crème brulee is luscious. Meet a favorite friend for lunch or dinner at Mat & Naddie's. They cater, too.

MY NEW ORLEANS DINING JOURNAL

<u>MICHAEL'S MID-CITY GRILL</u>

Date & Time:_____Total Expense: _____

Companion(s):_____

Description of décor:_____

Directions to restaurant
and parking information:_____

_____

Service:_____

Favorite Food(s)/Wine(s):_____

_____

_____

_____

_____

My remarks and
impressions:_____

_____

_____

_____

SAVE BUSINESS CARD OR RESTAURANT SOUVENIR HERE

MICHAEL'S MID-CITY GRILL

4139 Canal Boulevard
New Orleans, Louisiana 70119
(504) 486-8200

Mid-City
Moderate

Michael's is an eclectic Mid-City diner that offers a wide variety of eats for every palate. The atmosphere is relaxed and locals love this place for both casual business lunches or for dinner. Spacious booths line the dining room and there is also a bar that is a popular place to unwind after work. Michael's is one of the few places where locals begin to describe the restaurant by saying "They've got THE best _____." It's literally "fill in the blank."

For example, Ana thinks that this place has THE best place for crab claws. Ruth Ann thinks that "THE FRIED SHRIMP SANDWICH" is exactly that — THE best in the City and THE one and only. Of course, burgers, thick and of the hand-made variety are popular here as well as steaks, chicken, seafood and a variety of starters. Michael's is a place where the servers and customers know each other. It's a place where regulars are revered, can relax and order exactly what they've been craving all afternoon.

Check out the pictures on the wall which feature people who've ordered the "Big Bucks Burger." It claims to be the most expensive burger in America at $150 and is topped with sautéed mushrooms, sour cream, caviar, and comes with a bottle of Dom Perignon. I think some of these big bucks people look like they're on an expensive first date! Enjoy Michael's, it's a true local, New Orleans neighborhood kind of place.

MY NEW ORLEANS DINING JOURNAL

<u>MOSCA'S</u>

Date & Time:_____Total Expense: _____

Companion(s):_____

Description of décor:_____

Directions to restaurant
and parking information:_____

_____

Service:_____

Favorite Food(s)/Wine(s):_____

_____

_____

_____

_____

My remarks and
impressions:_____

_____

_____

_____

SAVE BUSINESS CARD OR RESTAURANT SOUVENIR HERE

MOSCA'S

4137 Highway 90 East
Avondale, Louisiana 70094
(504) 436-7743

Westbank
Moderate to Expensive

This Italian family-owned restaurant has thrived in the exact locale with the exact menu for nearly 50 years. Driving up to Mosca's feels a little like asking for directions at some old gas station on an infrequently traveled highway in the country. However, once you get past the shock that this IS the place your looking for, you're in store for an incredible eating experience.

Start by selecting a bottle of wine (there's a great selection of Italian red and whites). I always let them choose for me and I'm always pleased. As an entree, Mosca's Italian Oysters, Chicken a la Grande, and the Italian Shrimp are all equally fantastic and recommended. If you order the Italian shrimp (and I hope you do because they are not to be missed) be ready to get a little messy because peeled shrimp is never served peeled in Italy or at Mosca's. The spaghetti bordelaise is rich in flavors and a good accompaniment if you're ordering the chicken. For dessert, the pineapple fluff or cheesecake does the trick. At Mosca's you'll get a kick from the tiny glasses that the wines are served in and the un-matching chairs (sizes and styles) at each table. It seems as though there's been little thought given to redecorating or changing a thing since it opened. At Mosca's, we're glad they haven't changed a thing. This is a definite locals' secret and favorite place. Payment is cash only.

MY NEW ORLEANS DINING JOURNAL

MR. ED'S SEAFOOD & ITALIAN RESTAURANT

Date & Time:_____Total Expense: _____

Companion(s):_____

Description of décor:_____

Directions to restaurant
and parking information:_____

_____

Service:_____

Favorite Food(s)/Wine(s):_____

_____

_____

_____

_____

My remarks and
impressions:_____

_____

_____

_____

SAVE BUSINESS CARD OR RESTAURANT SOUVENIR HERE

MR. ED'S SEAFOOD & ITALIAN RESTAURANT

1001 Live Oak
Metairie, Louisiana 70005
(504) 838-0022

Bucktown
Moderate

Mr. Ed's is a casual, unassuming restaurant quietly tucked away in a neighborhood near the Lakefront. Tiffany, Hunter, and Emily love looking at the saltwater aquarium as they walk in on the left. Some locals make it a point to go to Mr. Ed's at least once a week with their aunt or uncle or nanan. The restaurant looks better than most neighborhood eateries and the food is definitely first rate.

My favorite is the fried soft-shell crab (when in season) and fried trout or red snapper. Their house specialties are Snapper Manda (sautéed snapper in a seasoned crawfish sauce served over pasta), shrimp-stuffed bell peppers (with crabmeat and crawfish), breaded or grilled pork chops, paneed veal with fettuccini, chicken fried steak, white or red beans, crawfish éttoufée, and pasta Orleans (Rigatoni pasta topped with crabmeat, shrimp, and crawfish in a cream sauce). Mr. Ed's Italian dishes are superb as well. Mr. Ed serves veal (topped with sautéed shrimp, lump crabmeat, or Marsala wine and mushrooms).

Most entrees run between $8 to $12 — you'll be totally satisfied with Mr. Eds. I think that's where we're going tonight.

MY NEW ORLEANS DINING JOURNAL

<u>NAUTICAL</u>

Date & Time:_____Total Expense: _____

Companion(s):_____

Description of décor:_____

Directions to restaurant
and parking information:_____

_____

Service:_____

Favorite Food(s)/Wine(s):_____

_____

_____

_____

_____

My remarks and
impressions:_____

_____

_____

_____

SAVE BUSINESS CARD OR RESTAURANT SOUVENIR HERE

NAUTICAL

7708 Maple Street
New Orleans, Louisiana 70118
(504) 866-7504

Uptown
Moderate to Expensive

Considering that this restaurant was voted by *Bon Apetit* as "Best New Restaurant New Orleans 1999" and that a local food critic voted it as "most romantic place to dine" (and also the fact that I recently had a dinner party there for Donald's birthday with 25 people), I voted this restaurant a *must do* experience.

All meals are prepared "from scratch" and seafood arrives daily. If you are looking for "fresh," this is the place. I personally and honestly rate this Uptown cozy bistro with ship paraphernalia and sailing décor as my number one choice for fresh seafood in the City. Must tries are (of course the outstanding fresh fish – don't fry mine please), the herb-roasted duckling (Maple Leaf Farms roasted semi-boneless duckling bathed in a sweet Merlot reduction sauce served with garlic mashed potatoes), crabmeat and Brie dip appetizer, and caramelized salmon with a herbed compound butter. Top off your dessert with a mouth-watering chocolate pecan truffle (served to all guests). Enjoy a fine bottle of wine while you take in the breezy, trendy atmosphere and courteous service from Nautical's crew. Eric Bay, the owner will make certain that your dining is smooth sailing all the way.

MY NEW ORLEANS DINING JOURNAL

<u>ODYSSEY GRILL</u>

Date & Time:_____Total Expense: _____

Companion(s):_____

Description of décor:_____

Directions to restaurant
and parking information:_____

_____

Service:_____

Favorite Food(s)/Wine(s):_____

_____

_____

_____

_____

My remarks and
impressions:_____

_____

_____

_____

SAVE BUSINESS CARD OR RESTAURANT SOUVENIR HERE

ODYSSEY GRILL

2037 Metairie Road
Metairie, Louisiana 70005
(504) 834-5775

Old Metairie
Moderate

Getting comfortable in its location on Metairie Road, Odyssey Grill continues to cook up a variety of mostly traditional Mediterranean and Aegean specialties. The spacious restaurant gives off a true feeling of a Greek tavern complete with artwork by a local Greek artist. Owner Rosita Skias takes pride in the fact that she uses the freshest ingredients, sticks to traditional recipes for the majority of dishes, and ends up serving good food that is healthful as well as classical.

A number of dips, cold and hot dishes, Lebanese and Greek combination platters start off as appetizers. These include traditional fare like hummus and taramosalata. Great is the roasted garlic soup, fried calamari appetizer, and mussels alla bianca. Entrees include specialties such as grilled octopus, whole grilled fish, moussaka, Moroccan chicken, and arni (roasted leg of lamb — cooked with garlic, oregano, and lemon juice). The shrimp souvlaki is served on a bed of rice with grilled vegetables. Odyssey Grill's Express Lunch Menu is offered Tuesday through Friday with its gourmet breakfast served on Saturday and Sunday 9 a.m. to 2 p.m. When locals are in the mood for Greek or Lebanese food, they stop by this neighborhood gem.

MY NEW ORLEANS DINING JOURNAL

<u>PERISTYLE</u>

Date & Time:_____Total Expense: _____

Companion(s):_____

Description of décor:_____

Directions to restaurant
and parking information:_____

_____

Service:_____

Favorite Food(s)/Wine(s):_____

_____

_____

_____

_____

My remarks and
impressions:_____

_____

_____

_____

SAVE BUSINESS CARD OR RESTAURANT SOUVENIR HERE

PERISTYLE

1041 Dumaine Street
New Orleans, Louisiana 70116
(504) 593-9535

French Quarter
Expensive   *Reservations Suggested*

Co-Owner's Thomas Sand, Jr. and Chef Anne Kearney Sand have turned this 19th century French Quarter building into a unique bistro that celebrates New Orleans style and cuisine. A mix of New Orleans and continental influences and an ever-changing and exciting menu make Peristlye one outstanding place to dine. The atmosphere includes two large murals that depict City Park circa 1905 and a gorgeous bar adorned with antique framed mirrors and antique mahogany. Shut down for some time due to a fire, Peristyle is back and better than ever.

Though the menu re-invents itself seasonally, some favorites are the Louisiana poached oysters, pheasant and artichoke ravioli, steamed mussels in a shellfish broth, sea scallops, filet mignon, and of course, any duck dish. The sweetbreads appetizer and crab salad are also a great way to get started. Not to miss is the flourless chocolate cake with burnt-sugar ice cream.

Peristyle is open for dinner only Tuesday through Saturday and for lunch on Friday only. Peristyle offers a very nice wine list and the service is excellent. Peristyle books up, so if you are planning to dine here, please call for reservations a couple of weeks ahead.

MY NEW ORLEANS DINING JOURNAL
<u>PHO TAU BAY RESTAURANT</u>

Date & Time:_____Total Expense: _____

Companion(s):_____

Description of décor:_____

Directions to restaurant
and parking information:_____

_____

Service:_____

Favorite Food(s)/Wine(s):_____

_____

_____

_____

_____

My remarks and
impressions:_____

_____

_____

_____

SAVE BUSINESS CARD OR RESTAURANT SOUVENIR HERE

PHO TAU BAY RESTAURANT

113-c Westbank Expressway	3116 N. Arnoult
Gretna, LA 70053	Metairie, LA 70002
(504) 368-9846	(504) 780-1063

Westbank/Metairie (2 locations)
Inexpensive

Pho Tau Bay is the place for authentic Vietnamese cuisine. Apart from the traditional Vietnamese fare, Pho Tau Bay serves such a wide variety of pho (soups) that it was hard to fit them onto only one menu. The exotic sweet and sour soup and the hot and spicy pork and beef soup are two favorites. You can also order a variety of appetizers and dishes to try and share guilt-free because everything you order here is beaming with freshness and plentiful, healthful ingredients. The Saigon Taco is stuffed full of bean sprouts, shrimp and pork and comes in a crispy thin tamarind shell, "Nuoc Mam" dressing (house specialty), and a basket of fresh herbs. It is eaten by tearing apart the taco and rewrapping it into lettuce leaves with fresh basil. The imperial egg rolls are deep-fried and stuffed with crabmeat, ground pork and vegetables. The steamed vermicelli patties are another favorite and come topped with such ingredients as chargrilled, sliced pork or pasted shrimp on sugar cane and are topped with grilled onions. Pho Tau Bay also offers its own twist on Southern po-boys with 10 different types of Vietnamese style po-boys.

Pho Tau Bay is open 365 days a year and opens its doors at 9 a.m. It closes promptly at 8:30 p.m. — so arrive early. If you get the chance to talk to Karl Sr. or Jr. — ask about the origins of the name "Pho Tau Bay" (literally meaning "soup airplane"); they tell a better story than I ever could here.

MY NEW ORLEANS DINING JOURNAL

PONTCHARTRAIN BISTRO AND WINE BAR
AT THE PONTCHARTRAIN HOTEL

Date & Time:_____Total Expense: _____

Companion(s):_____

Description of décor:_____

Directions to restaurant
and parking information:_____

_____

Service:_____

Favorite Food(s)/Wine(s):_____

_____

_____

_____

_____

My remarks and
impressions:_____

_____

_____

_____

SAVE BUSINESS CARD OR RESTAURANT SOUVENIR HERE

PONTCHARTRAIN BISTRO AND WINE BAR
AT THE PONTCHARTRAIN HOTEL

2031 St. Charles Avenue
New Orleans, Louisiana 70140
(504) 524-0581 / 1-800-777-6193

Uptown
Moderate to Expensive

Located in the heart of the Garden District at the historic Pontchartrain Hotel, the beautifully renovated Pontchartrain Bistro and Wine Bar is a New Orleans tradition for local power breakfasts and lunches. Jazz music quietly accompanies your meal and you are reminded that this is not only the South, but also New Orleans, a city that demands respect for its style and good taste. Dinner at the Pontchartrain Bistro and Wine Bar offers a comfortable and romantic setting.

The renovations in September 2000 brought forth a welcome surprise with hand-painted, wooden ceiling beams (originally painted nearly a century earlier) and reflect the original French Provincial style of the hotel and restaurant.

Chef Harvey Loumiet's menus reflect the dramatic and yet casual French décor with changing menus for breakfast, lunch, and dinner. The menu ranges from traditional New Orleans cuisine to the new and innovative – exemplified in such appetizer dishes as seafood and fried green tomato Napoleon and duck with wild mushroom confit en crepe to entrees such as grilled double cut pork chop with Parmesan polenta and a cranberry demi-glace. There are also a number of daily specials off the menu.

MY NEW ORLEANS DINING JOURNAL

PUPUSERIA DIVINO CORAZON

Date & Time:_____Total Expense: _____

Companion(s):_____

Description of décor:_____

Directions to restaurant
and parking information:_____

_____

Service:_____

Favorite Food(s)/Wine(s):_____

_____

_____

_____

_____

My remarks and
impressions:_____

_____

_____

_____

SAVE BUSINESS CARD OR RESTAURANT SOUVENIR HERE

PUPUSERIA DIVINO CORAZON

2300 Belle Chasse Highway
Gretna, Louisiana 70053
(504) 368-5724

Westbank
Inexpensive

If you don't know what a Pupusa is, once you eat here, you will. Owned by Salvadorans, this Westbank restaurant serves up Central American and Mexican dishes at great prices and in an environment similar to that in Central America. The lively dining room is decorated with pictures of the Sacred Heart and other religious pictures and memorabilia from El Salvador. Casual dining, great prices and meals fresh-cooked to order, make this place a favorite of locals (both Hispanic and non-Hispanic).

I first discovered what Pupusas were while traveling in San Salvador and I must admit that I became hooked on them. I can best describe Pupusas as a sort of corn or flour tortilla that is filled with either cheese, pork, onions, etc., then chargrilled. Sounds simple, but there's more . . . something special happens when the cheese overflows from the tortilla and then gets crunchy on the outside — and that something is delicious! As you can see, it's one of those things that's a little difficult to describe. And there's more, Pupusas are eaten with a spicy marinated salad.

Apart from Pupusas, Salvadorans make their own special brand of chicken tamales with ingredients that often include green olives and potatoes. There are a number of Mexican-style dishes that come in good size portions. Another Salvadoran dish that people like are the tamal de elote con crème. Salpicon con consommé (beef broiled in stock) and other daily specials are not to be missed.

MY NEW ORLEANS DINING JOURNAL

<u>REGINELLI'S PIZZERIA</u>

Date & Time:_____Total Expense: _____

Companion(s):_____

Description of décor:_____

Directions to restaurant
and parking information:_____

_____

Service:_____

Favorite Food(s)/Wine(s):_____

_____

_____

_____

_____

My remarks and
impressions:_____

_____

_____

_____

SAVE BUSINESS CARD OR RESTAURANT SOUVENIR HERE

REGINELLI'S PIZZERIA
(3 Locations)

Uptown
741 State Street
New Orleans, LA 70118
(504) 899-1414

Lakeview
874 Harrison Avenue
New Orleans, LA 70124
(504) 488-1033

Harahan
5608 Citrus Boulevard
Harahan, LA 70123
(504) 818-0111

Uptown/Lakeview/Harahan
Inexpensive

Reginelli's is a neighborhood pizzeria with a new take on the traditional pizza that has gained the restaurant popularity with both locals and college students alike. All pizzas are made fresh — from scratch — and are not shy of loads of toppings. Also offered are a range of fresh, creative salads and appetizers to mouth-watering focaccia, pita press sandwiches, calzones, and stuffed pasta dishes.

Appetizers include such delectables as baked Brie calzone, topped with sun-dried pear chutney and baked polenta topped with spicy shrimp and pancetta cream sauce. The salads come in generous portions and can be a meal in themselves. Pizzas come in two sizes. You may order the specialty pizzas that are the chef's design or even design a pizza of your own. Some of the custom toppings available include roasted garlic, sun dried tomatoes, shrimp, chicken, calamata olives, or new potatoes, as well as a variety of cheese and traditional pizza toppings. The specialty pizza "Veggie Roast" is made with large roasted garlic heads, roasted eggplant, Gorgonzola cheese, mozzarella cheese, and spicy roasted red pepper sauce. It's a favorite, as well as the rosemary chicken focaccia sandwich, asparagus pita, and fontina toast.

Reginelli's is open seven days a week and for those lucky enough to live in the neighborhood, they deliver.

MY NEW ORLEANS DINING JOURNAL

<u>SANTA FE</u>

Date & Time:_____Total Expense: _____

Companion(s):_____

Description of décor:_____

Directions to restaurant
and parking information:_____

_____

Service:_____

Favorite Food(s)/Wine(s):_____

_____

_____

_____

_____

My remarks and
impressions:_____

_____

_____

_____

SAVE BUSINESS CARD OR RESTAURANT SOUVENIR HERE

SANTA FE

801 Frenchmen Street
New Orleans, Louisiana 70116
(504) 944-6854

French Quarter
Moderate

The creations at this French Quarter Mexican restaurant are so enticing that it's been a favorite of locals for many years now. Fresh ingredients begin the fusion here. There are few chef's in the City that escape the temptation to see what happens when they put together the City's wonderful cuisine traditions with the ingredients and styling of their choice. Santa Fe is no exception. What develops is a new take on the food of Mexico we all know and crave. This time it's Creole, Italian-influenced Mexican, the outcome of which is nothing short of fantastic. The restaurant feels young, hip, and lively (and a good place to get together with friends). The frozen margaritas at Santa Fe are notorious for both their flavor and their punch.

Some of Santa Fe's fare include gypsy fajitas, chicken maximillian (stuffed with Asadero cheese and chorizo), tamales with chipolte-seasoned pork, crayfish fajitas (among others), delicious nachos, and other dishes that all come in more than adequate portions. After dinner, the Chef (who is German) has some wonderful European desserts to offer. They are both eye-candy and delicious. Santa Fe gets crowded, so it is best to go early or make a reservation. Even with reservations, there is a wait sometimes. However, the waiting area is cool and comfortable, and if you order a margarita or two, you won't feel a thing.

MY NEW ORLEANS DINING JOURNAL

<u>TAJ MAHAL INDIAN CUISINE</u>

Date & Time:_____Total Expense: _____

Companion(s):_____

Description of décor:_____

Directions to restaurant
and parking information:_____

_____

Service:_____

Favorite Food(s)/Wine(s):_____

_____

_____

_____

_____

My remarks and
impressions:_____

_____

_____

_____

SAVE BUSINESS CARD OR RESTAURANT SOUVENIR HERE

TAJ MAHAL INDIAN CUISINE
923 Metairie Road
Metairie, Louisiana 70005
(504) 836-6859

Old Metairie
Moderate

The Keswani family, who have years of successful restaurant experience in New Orleans, manage to serve up (once again) authentic and delicious Indian Cuisine. This hidden Metairie space makes its patrons feel privileged to a guilty hidden pleasure discovery. Nestled off Metairie Road, you could almost miss this place if you didn't know it existed. Once inside, you feel like you've discovered a small jewel. The place is decorated with beautiful Indian art and lushness. Indian Music completes the setting where aromas rule and India's complexity and beauty are successfully transplanted.

The lunch buffet is recommended, provided you're in the mood to sample and fill-up. Indian food always makes me feel strangely relaxed — especially the evening hours. The menu is filled with an array of Indian regional dishes and plenty of appetizers, soups, salads, vegetarian dishes (so many here, I think that any vegetarian — or person who just loves vegetables — would be delighted). Traditional curry dishes that are served with rice, raita, and katchumber, tandoori oven specialties, pre-arranged diverse dinners for two (a good way to sample a lot of things you might not otherwise be brave enough to try), biryanis, breads and complex, mouth-watering desserts are just a few of the exotic treasures at Taj Mahal.

If you're craving Indian food, you will most surely find something here to fill your cravings. If you're uptown and having cravings, try Nirvana on Magazine . . . same ownership and also really good.

MY NEW ORLEANS DINING JOURNAL

<u>THE PELICAN CLUB</u>

Date & Time:_____Total Expense: _____

Companion(s):_____

Description of décor:_____

Directions to restaurant
and parking information:_____

_____

Service:_____

Favorite Food(s)/Wine(s):_____

_____

_____

_____

_____

My remarks and
impressions:_____

_____

_____

_____

SAVE BUSINESS CARD OR RESTAURANT SOUVENIR HERE

THE PELICAN CLUB

312 Exchange Alley
New Orleans, Louisiana 70130
(504) 523-1504

French Quarter
Expensive   *Reservations Suggested*

Tucked away in Exchange Alley in the French Quarter is a surprising upscale restaurant with innovative cooking that combines a flair of the East with Southeast Louisiana influences. Although its in the French Quarter and tourists do manage to find this place, it remains a favorite local/romantic spot. The food is engaging (as is your dining companion, hopefully) and the atmosphere is sophisticated and warm. In other words, The Pelican Club is one of those restaurants you'd feel good about putting on your favorite outfit and hopping by for dinner aprés-theatre or an arts event.

Popular appetizers are the spring rolls, seafood martini, and escargot. Main dishes that rule are the Cajun jambalaya that has chicken, andouille, shrimp and mussels, seafood fricassee (fish scallops, shrimp, mussels, clams and lobster served with Louisiana risotto), and roasted filet mignon with wild mushrooms and garlic fricassee with Madeira demi-glace. The wait staff prides itself on its knowledge of details. A pianist plays requests on Friday and Saturday nights (7 – 10 p.m.). The Pelican Club is open for dinner only and reservations are suggested. The Pelican Club has more than a few feathers in its cap including, the *Wine Spectator's* "award of excellence" (seven years in a row) and rated four beans by the *Times Picayune* with further accolades from *Condé Nast Traveler* and others.

MY NEW ORLEANS DINING JOURNAL

THE SPORTING HOUSE CAFE

Date & Time:_____Total Expense: _____

Companion(s):_____

Description of décor:_____

Directions to restaurant
and parking information:_____

_____

Service:_____

Favorite Food(s)/Wine(s):_____

_____

_____

_____

_____

My remarks and
impressions:_____

_____

_____

_____

SAVE BUSINESS CARD OR RESTAURANT SOUVENIR HERE

THE SPORTING HOUSE CAFÉ
916 Lafayette Street
New Orleans, Louisiana 70113
(504) 561-1216

Central Business District
Moderate

Breakfast/Lunch Only
and Private Party

This stylish little café housed in a historic townhouse that was, in former times, a brothel catering to local politicians and a gentlemen's sporting club offers creative lunchtime fun and fare. Playing upon the history of the building, Owner/Chef David Duggins, Jr., has created a diverse menu with dishes of amusingly titled creations served in an atmosphere that reflects and celebrates the elegance and decadence of New Orleans at the turn-of-the-century.

Foreplay (appetizers) include "Naked Onion soup au Gratin" and "Pussy fingers" (Catfish fingers). Po-boys include the "Gobbler and Gomorrah" (roasted turkey with melted Swiss, caper-Creole dijonnaise, lettuce, tomatoes, and onions on French bread), "Oyster Faux Pas" (oysters on a bed of spinach and Brie cheese sprinkled with balsamic), "Busty Beef," and "Shrimp Satchmo." The "Ladies of the Green" (salads) include the "Naughty Senorita," "Miss Rena's Racy Shrimp Salad," the "Infamous Lulu White" (house recommended), "Oysters Orgy," and "Madame Butterfly Salad."

The Sporting House Café is open for lunch and breakfast *only* and on Wednesdays through Fridays for happy hour cocktails. A different "celebrity bartender" hosts each Wednesday and shoulder massages are available in the "Quickie Room." Interesting historic photos and memorabilia are displayed in the main dining room, back parlor, and powder room. The Sporting House Café is a great place to have lunch and experience a bit of history with old New Orleans fun.

MY NEW ORLEANS DINING JOURNAL

TONY ANGELLO'S RESTAURANT

Date & Time:_____Total Expense: _____

Companion(s):_____

Description of décor:_____

Directions to restaurant
and parking information:_____

_____

Service:_____

Favorite Food(s)/Wine(s):_____

_____

. _____

_____

_____

My remarks and
impressions:_____

_____

_____

_____

SAVE BUSINESS CARD OR RESTAURANT SOUVENIR HERE

TONY ANGELLO'S RESTAURANT

6262 Fleur De Lis Drive
New Orleans, Louisiana 70124
(504) 488-0888

Lakeview   *Reservations Suggested*
Moderate to Expensive

Housed in a ranch-style corner home in West Lakeview, Tony Angello's is, for many, the only place to go when you want to eat authentic Sicilian Cuisine. There is the menu, of course, where you can order individual courses, but what most locals love here is to request the "feed me" option. The "feed me" can produce numerous smaller size portions of a variety of dishes served at Tony Angello's.

It's a wonderful eating experience that's both an exciting and interesting way to try it all. But, be sure to include space in your tummy as well as some extra time. Just getting through the appetizers can take up to an hour. Since I have nearly always ordered this way, I think it's the only way to eat at Tony Angello's. However, when appetite and time are a restraint, by all means, order from the menu.

The marinara sauce is authentic and sides come with nearly every entrée. Favorites are the Osso Bucco, any of the veal dishes, rabbit, quail, and seafood. Many also love the Eggplant Tina. Sure bets for getting your mouth watering are the oysters Bienville or Rockefeller and the lobster cup. I also love the way they do fish here – perfect! The atmosphere at Tony Angello's is relaxed and warm. Tony Angelo's remains popular and a true Lakeview find.

MY NEW ORLEANS DINING JOURNAL

<u>UGLESICH RESTAURANT & BAR</u>

Date & Time:_____Total Expense: _____

Companion(s):_____

Description of décor:_____

Directions to restaurant
and parking information:_____

_____

Service:_____

Favorite Food(s)/Wine(s):_____

_____

_____

_____

_____

My remarks and
impressions:_____

_____

_____

_____

SAVE BUSINESS CARD OR RESTAURANT SOUVENIR HERE

UGLESICH RESTAURANT & BAR

1238 Baronne Street
New Orleans, Louisiana 70113
(504) 523-5871 • (504) 525-4925

Downtown
Expensive

This lunch-only place isn't groomed for beauty. As you drive up to the restaurant the outside of the restaurant definitely does not accurately reflect the religious dining experience of truly scrumptious flavors awaiting your palate. There's a small humble dining room — beverage crates line the walls giving it a blue-collar dive motif. Go early (or wait — worth any long wait). The menu is filled with seafood dishes — lots of them — like oyster, shrimp, crawfish, and crabmeat appetizers. Try the oysters fresh or fried (with Bleu cheese in the batter). The oyster shucker at the bar (voted one of the best schuckers in the City[1]) mixes his own cocktail sauce that is not shy on horseradish or Tabasco. Trout Anthony is a must — and the fried green tomatoes are authentically Southern topped with shrimp. Some of their creations include Voodoo Shrimp (an Asian Creole-inspired dish), soft-shell crab, and crawfish Maque Choux (crawfish smothered with white corn and tomatoes). Be prepared to spend around $40 for two people. Should the menu overwhelm you with indecision, ask the owners (Anthony & Gail) (probably your waiter) to guide you to something succulent.

---

[1] Only in New Orleans would there be a contest for shucking oysters!

MY NEW ORLEANS DINING JOURNAL

VINCENT'S ITALIAN CUISINE/VINCENT'S

Date & Time:_____Total Expense: _____

Companion(s):_____

Description of décor:_____

Directions to restaurant
and parking information:_____

_____

Service:_____

Favorite Food(s)/Wine(s):_____

_____

_____

_____

_____

My remarks and
impressions:_____

_____

_____

_____

SAVE BUSINESS CARD OR RESTAURANT SOUVENIR HERE

VINCENT'S ITALIAN CUISINE/VINCENT'S

7839 St. Charles Avenue	4411 Chastant Street
New Orleans, LA 70118	Metairie, LA 70006
(504) 866-9313	(504) 885-2984

Uptown/Metairie
Moderate

After years of restaurant experience, owner Vincent Catalanotto decided to give the restaurant business a shot on his own. Beginning with the original location in Metairie (and now with a second location on St. Charles Avenue), Vincent's serves up some truly great Northern Italian fare in a familiar, neighborhood-style atmosphere.   Vincent's is the type of place where all emphasis is put on the cooking and that's exactly what locals appreciate. The Uptown location is smaller than the one in Metairie, but just as tasty.

Some of the favorites at Vincent's are the garlic chicken, Osso Bucco, crabmeat and corn bisque soup, blackened tuna, sautéed trout (served with a crabmeat topping), the cannelloni (stuffed with veal, spinach and cheese), and all the veal dishes. Lunch specials this week included jumbo shrimp Parmesan, redfish with crabmeat cream sauce, and an eggplant dish. Mr. Catalanotto is wonderful at fixing sauces and creating original spins on classic favorites.   The Tiramisu is a great choice for dessert. Vincent's is open for lunch and dinner. Bring your appetite and love for all things Italian!

MY NEW ORLEANS DINING JOURNAL

<u>ZACHARY'S RESTAURANT</u>

Date & Time:_____Total Expense: _____

Companion(s):_____

Description of décor:_____

Directions to restaurant
and parking information:_____

_____

Service:_____

Favorite Food(s)/Wine(s):_____

_____

_____

_____

_____

My remarks and
impressions:_____

_____

_____

_____

SAVE BUSINESS CARD OR RESTAURANT SOUVENIR HERE

ZACHARY'S RESTAURANT
8400 Oak Street
New Orleans, Louisiana 70118
(504) 865-1559

Uptown
Moderate

Mr. Baquet calls his place the only "Creole soul food" place in the City and talks proudly about the traditions of good cooking. Our conversation naturally yields to their crispy fried chicken passed down from his father, Eddie Baquet who ran the soul food restaurant Eddie's. Nestled on Oak Street, a warm, spacious house has been turned into Zachary's dining mecca. When you enter from the patio door, you'll see that there's a sophisticated bar that looks like an inviting place for a cocktail. The dining rooms have a roomy and slightly tropical feeling.

For lunchtime, Zachary's is a great place to go. The buffet is not only really excellent but also a good value at less than $9.00. Last time I visited Zachary's, the lunch buffet included rich seafood gumbo, white beans, andouille sausage, fried chicken, greens, broiled catfish, fresh green beans, and some great bread pudding. I won't admit to the number of times I filled up the plate, but I wasn't the only one at the table to do so. So, I figured who's looking! My sister and I took our friend Souzan here for her birthday. Souzan loved Zachary's food and atmosphere!

For dinner, Zachary's rules. The Trout Baquet with lump crabmeat and the pork chops are local favorites. Locals also love the seafood platter and roast beef brisket. Just about everything at Zachary's is great and if you're having trouble choosing what to order, the wait staff is very friendly and helpful. Next time we go to Zachary's, I think I'll try to dine in the Jazz room (I like the happy, fuschia pink walls). Zachary's is soul food with style, tradition, and individuality.

DEBBY'S SEAFOOD GUMBO

1/4 c. vegetable oil
5 tbsp. flour
1 large chopped yellow onion
1 c. chopped celery
1/4 c. chopped parsley
(fresh or dried)
1/2 c. shallot tops
5 or 6 chopped garlic cloves
1 c. chopped green pepper
2 cans tomatoe sauce
1 c. chopped tomatoes
2 lbs. fresh sliced okra
3 lbs. large fresh (raw)
peeled & deveined
shrimp
2-1/2 qts. water
1 tbsp. black pepper
Salt to taste

2 tbsp. Tony Chachere's
Original Seasoning
2 tbsp. dried onions
1 tsp. sugar
1 bay leaf
1 lb. lump crabmeat
3 fresh gumbo crabs (pull
claws off, remove hard
shell, remove lungs and
orange stuff), then break
in quarters (use claws,
and quarter parts).
3 doz. oysters
1 tbsp. gumbo filé powder

(Make a roux by placing oil in a 7-8 quart heavy cast iron skillet - heat and gradually stir in flour. Cook on medium heat until flour is dark brown. This may take up to 20 minutes.) Add the fresh onion, green pepper, shallot tops, parsley, celery, and garlic. (You may add a bit of water if it is too dry at this point.) Stir constantly and continue cooking for about 10 minutes. Vegetables should be lightly browned at this point. Add tomato sauce, chopped tomatoes, and okra. Cook slowly, adding 2 to 3 cups of cold water—a little at a time. Add the rest of the water. Add seasonings: salt, dried onions, black pepper, sugar, bay leaf, gumbo filé, and Tony Chachere's Original Seasoning. Add gumbo crabs. Raise the heat slightly and bring the mixture to a quick boil then immediately lower to simmer for about an hour stirring occasionally to prevent sticking to the bottom of pot (adding water if necessary). Fifteen minutes before serving add shrimp and crabmeat. Simmer until the shrimp turn pink. Add oysters after heat is off and approximately five minutes before serving. Serve over brown or white or brown steamed rice.

TRADITIONAL NEW ORLEANS
RED BEANS & RICE

2 lbs. dry red kidney beans
1 medium yellow onion finely chopped
1 c. finely chopped celery
1 pound of ham seasoning (I buy a small whole ham
    and slice in cubes.)
5 garlic cloves minced
1 large bay leaf
Salt, cayenne and black pepper
6 – 8 c. water
1 can of tomato puree
1 lb. beef sausage

Wash and soak beans overnight. In a large pot, boil water with ham seasoning for about 20 minutes. Add beans, onions, garlic, celery, bay leaf, tomato puree, and pepper. Reduce heat and simmer for approximately three to five hours until beans are tender. To make creamy gravy, remove one cup of cooked beans and blend in a blender. Add back to pot and stir. Add sausage, salt, pepper, and cayenne pepper to taste. Serve over hot white or brown rice.

OYSTERS PARMESAN

1 large yellow or Vidalia onion, minced
5 cloves garlic, minced
1/2 c. extra virgin olive oil
1 pint of raw oysters with liquid
1-1/4 c. seasoned breadcrumbs
1/4 c. grated Parmesan cheese
4 strips of bacon, crumbled

Sauté onion and garlic in olive oil until slightly brown; add oysters and cook until the edges of the oysters curl. Remove from heat; stir in breadcrumbs, cheese, oyster liquid and bacon. Mix well. The mixture should be of a very moist consistency, similar to stuffing. Bake in individual greased casseroles at 350 degrees for 30 minutes. Yields 4 servings.

CRABMEAT RUBY

1 c. yellow onion finely
1/3 c. celery chopped fine
1/4 lb. butter
1 tsp. sage
1 tsp. nutmeg
1/2 cut of minced parsley
2 tbsp. mayonnaise
1 tbsp. Worcestershire Sauce
1 can Campbell's cream of mushroom soup
3/4 c. Sherry
1 pound white crabmeat
3 c. crushed potato chips

Sauté onions and celery in butter until onions are wilted. Stir in crabmeat and seasonings. Mix well. Add mushroom soup, sherry, Worcestershire Sauce, mayonnaise, and crabmeat mixture. Place in casserole or individual ramekins. Sprinkle with finely crushed potato chips. Bake 30 minutes in a 350 degree oven until bubbly and nicely browned.

OYSTERS ORLEANS

4 doz. raw oysters
1-1/2 c. Italian bread crumbs
1/4 c. olive oil
4 tbsp. bacon fat
1/2 c. Parmesan Cheese
1/4 c. water

Water from oysters
6 cloves garlic, sautéed
Pinch of salt, black pepper
    and cayenne pepper
1 green onion finely
    chopped

Mix breadcrumbs and Parmesan cheese together. Add olive oil and juice from oysters and melted bacon fat, garlic, salt, pepper, green onion and cayenne. Let stand and give crumbs a chance to absorb all moisture (approximately 10-15 minutes). (If too dry, add water; if too soggy, add more bread crumbs.) Mix in oysters. Place in shallow pan and bake in hot oven 20-25 minutes at 325 degrees. Serves 8.

BBQ SHRIMP

2 lbs. large uncooked shrimp with vein removed
1 c. BBQ sauce
1 stick of butter
1/2 c. extra virgin olive oil
5 garlic cloves finely chopped
1 green onion finely chopped
Crushed black pepper
Salt
Garlic powder
Whole fresh rosemary leaves

Place shrimp in a shallow pan. Mix rest of ingredients and pour over shrimp overnight. Place in oven under broiler until shrimp turn pink. Place in oven lowering temperature to 350 degrees until thoroughly cooked (about 5 – 10 minutes.)

SHRIMP STUFFED MIRLITONS

4 mirlitons
1/2 stick butter
1 onion, minced
4 cloves garlic, minced
1/2 c. celery, chopped
Salt and pepper to taste
1/2 tsp. dry mustard

1-1/2 c. bread crumbs
1 egg
1 lb. shrimp (sautéed in
    butter and garlic)
1/2 c. sharp cheese
    (optional)
Buttered bread crumbs

Wash and cut mirlitons in half, lengthwise or leave whole. Cover with cold water and bring to a boil. Simmer for 30 minutes until tender. Remove from water and cool. Remove the seed and discard. Carefully scoop out the soft pulp of the mirliton, leaving the skin unbroken. Set the shells aside. Chop or mash mirliton pulp. Soak bread in milk. In a skillet, sauté the onion, garlic, and celery. Add merliton, breadcrumbs, salt, pepper, shrimp, egg, and cheese. Cook for about 5 minutes. Remove from fire. Fill shells with stuffing, top with buttered breadcrumbs and bake at 350 degrees for 20 minutes until crumbs are brown.

CREAMY PRALINES

3 c. sugar
1 c. buttermilk
1/4 c. Karo syrup

1 tsp. baking soda
3 c. pecans

Mix ingredients in deep boiler and boil until soft ball stage. Turn off fire and add 1 teaspoon of baking soda and 1 teaspoon of vanilla. Return to fire and bring to boil (about 1 minute). (The soda causes the sugar mix to foam.) Remove from heat and add 3 cups of pecans and beat until creamy (about 5 minutes). Pour with spoon on wax paper until cool.

PECAN PIE

1/2 c. sugar
1 pinch salt
1 stick butter
3 eggs

1 c. white Karo syrup
2 tbsp. flour
1 c. whole pecans
1 tsp. vanilla

Mix ingredients as in order. Put in unbaked pie shell. Bake 35-40 minutes at 350 degrees or until brown.

BREAD PUDDING

3 c. stale French bread, crumbled
1 c. melted butter
1 c. whole milk
7 eggs
1-1/2 c. sugar
1 tbsp. pure vanilla extract
1/2 c. raisins

Preheat oven to 350 degrees. Soak bread in milk until soft. Beat eggs. Mid eggs and rest of ingredients in large bowl. Place in a greased baking dish. Set baking dish in pan of hot water. Bake at 350 degrees for about 1 hour.

BREAD PUDDING SAUCE

1 box powdered sugar
1 tsp. pure vanilla
1/4 cup rum
1/2 stick softened butter
Whole Milk *(added to make sauce thinner)*

Mix sugar, vanilla, rum, and softened butter (add milk as needed). Heat in a double boiler on stove until warmed enough to pour over hot bread pudding.

PLANTATION CREPES

2 eggs
2/3 c. milk
2 tbsp. melted butter
1/2 tsp. vanilla

1/2 c. all-purpose flour
2 tsp. confectioners sugar
1/4 tsp. salt

Beat eggs well, add milk, melted butter and vanilla. Sift together flour, sugar and salt and add to milk mixture beating until smooth. Butter a small 6 or 7 inch skillet and heat over medium heat until very hot. Pour about 2 tablespoons of batter into skillet, tilting pan to cover bottom. Fry until lightly browned; turn and brown on other side. Stack crepes and keep them warm until ready to serve. (Makes 12 crepes.)

SAUCE FOR PLANTATION CREPES

5 tbsp. butter
5 tbsp. confectioners
   sugar
Thin peeling from one
   orange

Thin peeling from one lemon
Juice of one orange
1/4 c. warm Brandy
4 tbsp. Curacao

Melt butter in chafing dish or electric skillet. Add orange and lemon peels and cook, stirring until soft and transparent, about 3 - 5 minutes. Remove peels and discard. Add the orange juice and Curacao and heat. Roll or fold crepes into quarters and add to sauce, basting and heating thoroughly. Pour warm Brandy over all, ignite and baste crepes with blazing sauce. When the flame dies serve crepes topped with sauce.

A Cajun Grandmother's Recipes . . .

My Grandmother was, and still is, one of my favorite cooks. She grew up and raised her four children in Lafayette, Louisiana, the heart of Acadian Louisiana. My grandparents were both from big families and grew up with French as their first language. Both of my grandparents could trace their family roots in Louisiana back to the late 1600's, early 1700's. Cooking and bragging about her grandchildren were my grandmother's favorite past times. There was always something prepared and ready to eat in her kitchen. About a year before her passing, she gave me a few of her recipes. She was not one to measure or follow anyone's directions. The recipes are given here exactly as she told them to me. Feel free to adjust the quantity of ingredients according to your taste. This is what she also suggested. This is the way Cajun women pass down their recipes and keep them alive. Each generation is free to prepare these dishes as they like. I am proud to have these recipes and to be able to pass them on to you.

Jamie Menutis